Other Days Around Me

Above
A once-typical scene at London Apprentice on Whit Monday afternoon. Sunday School scholars of New Mills
Primitive Methodist Chapel would march behind a local band to their sports and tea treat. (Harry Stark)

Back cover
A view from the south towards the former "Iron Bridge" at Tregorrick.

Harry Stark c. 1922

Other Days Around Me

Early Memories of
St. Austell and the Pentewan Valley
as recorded by Harry Stark

Published by D.J. Stark

Other Days Around Me

ISBN   0   9531704   0   3

First published 1997 by
D.J. Stark, Orchard Lodge,
London Apprentice, St. Austell,
Cornwall, PL26 7AR.
Tel. 01726 75423

Printed
by
Swift Print
104 Treverbyn Road,
St. Austell, PL25 4EW.
Tel. 01726 70700

CONTENTS

ACKNOWLEDGEMENTS

In compiling this book, I am indebted to the following people who have been pleased to allow me to use their personal photographs and memorabilia:-

Mrs. A. Armstrong
Mr. W.O. Brown
Mr. S. Cloke
Mr. L.M. Coon
Mr. R.E. Evans
Miss J. Hambley
Mr. J.W. Hocking
Mrs. D.M. Matthews
Mrs. A. Stone
Mr. V.K. Tonkin

I am grateful to the following companies which have given me permission to use their picture-postcards:-

Ian Allan Group Ltd., Shepperton, Middx., TW17 8AS.
Fine Art Developments Plc., Bradford, W. Yorks, BD4 6HW.
The Francis Frith Collection, Shaftesbury, Dorset, SP7 8AT.
Hunting Aerofilms Ltd., Boreham Wood, Herts., WD6 1EJ.
National Railway Museum, York, YO2 4XJ.
W.H. Smith Group Plc., London, EC1N 6SN.

I am also grateful to The Cornish Guardian and to The West Briton for permitting me to reproduce extracts from their newspapers, to the Cornish Studies Library and Plymouth Central Library for the help given, and to the Editor of the Journal of The Federation of Old Cornwall Societies for the use of the poems.

My special thanks go to my brother, Ken, for the encouragement given to our father at the time and for typing his notes on a portable typewriter all those years ago, and to my wife, Carole, and my son, James, for the subsequent word processing and photography, and for their unstinting help in so many ways.

I have endeavoured to trace all holders of copyright and I apologise to anyone who has inadvertently not been acknowledged.

FOREWORD

My father, Harry Stark, was born in 1898, in a cottage on Menagwins Farm, where his father, John, was employed as an agricultural labourer. This cottage, which still exists, was formerly the Count House and Mine Office to Menagwins Mine. Menagwins Mine, also known as East Polgooth Mine, was in its heyday between 1852 and 1855. He attended St. Austell Central School at West Hill and in his early teens he went to work for Mr. Frederick Cole (later Cole & George), who ran a small farm and butchery business at Tregorrick. There he learned his trade as a butcher with this family business, in whose employment he remained for a period of forty-two years, except for army service during the First World War. When this firm ceased trading, Harry found employment as a storeman with Farm Industries Ltd. at East Hill, St. Austell.

Upon the death of his mother in 1929, he purchased a pair of cottages and some land at London Apprentice, and, after a few years, married Miss Lilian Yelland from Carclaze. The couple built a new house in the village and Harry lived there until his death in 1981. They had three children - myself, my sister Jennifer, and my brother Kenneth.

About a year before his death, he decided to record his earliest memories of life and work in and around the market town of St. Austell and the Pentewan Valley, which he loved, and where he had lived and worked for nearly eighty-three years. Fortunately, he owned a box-camera and several of the photographs included in this book are those he took in the 1920's and 1930's. I have supplemented his photographs with old picture-postcards from my own collection, and with others kindly loaned to me, which illustrate his text. I have also included, by way of annotation, information obtained from various sources which I hope will enhance his memories and provide further interest.

My father was a passionate Cornishman and throughout his life he maintained a keen interest in the people he knew and the places he loved. This is reflected in the notes he made, which I hope you, the reader, will find as interesting as I still do after having read them many times. My greatest regret now is not having made time to have gleaned more information from him. Nowadays, there is a growing trend of people investigating local social and topographical history, and I have, therefore, included a few comments, and captions to the photographs which I hope will add further interest to his monograph.

DAVID STARK
August, 1997

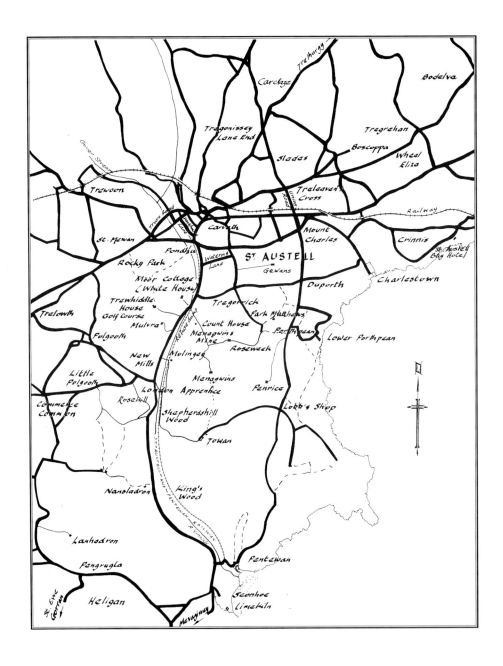

PREFACE

Anyone wishing to find a documented and authoritative history of St. Austell may be disillusioned by the contents herein, for the purpose of these notes is not to provide such details, but merely to recall some of the activities and changes which I have witnessed over my eighty-two years, all of which have been spent in this area. I can lay no claim to be an historian or accomplished writer, but I hope the reader may be entertained by the script. I can only say that it has been an enormous pleasure to recall the events, and I pay tribute to those older people of the area who have spurred me on to complete it. I make little reference to information which can be found in other accounts of St. Austell, preferring to concentrate on the extent of my own memories.

HARRY STARK
January, 1980

Oft, in the stilly night,
Ere Slumber's chain has bound me,
Sweet Memory brings the light
Of other days around me.

THOMAS MOORE
(National Airs 1815)

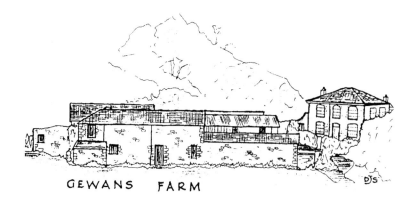

GEWANS FARM

The Road to Menagwins

There's an old green road, an old, old road -
Few know where it now begins -
That runs for a mile with never a stile
From Gewans to Menagwins;
An old and rambling packhorse track
That is level in parts and wide,
But strait and steep where it valleys deep
In the heart of the countryside.

'Tis a lovely way in the month of May,
In Spring, when the growth is rife
After the showers and a myriad of flowers
Are humming with insect life;
Winding down through the sunlit woods
That lend to the golden rays
The faery sheen of a leafy screen
O'er a glimmering bluebell haze.

'Tis a lovely way on a summer's day
In the vale, where it dips and turns
From an open glade to the welcome shade
And coolth of the moss and ferns
'Tis a lovely way on a rainy day
When the hedges are green again;
And the scent of the wood is sweet and good
After the rain !

But in Autumn time, in the morning time,
I love it the best of all
When the sunbeams tryst with a rising mist
And tints on the foliage fall !
When dewdrops glisten in rainbow hues
Where the gossamer spider spins
Down the old green road,
The old, old road,
From Gewans to Menagwins.

E.T. BOND

*(First published in **Old Cornwall** - The Journal
of the Federation of Old Cornwall Societies
Vol. IV, No. 4, Summer 1945.)*

*Mr. W.O. Brown of Menagwins kindly allowed a photograph to be taken of this painting. He confirmed
that my father had told him that he could remember the house being rebuilt in the early 1900's. Some
granite-mullioned windows from the former building have been incorporated into the present farmhouse,
as has a stone bearing the inscription RBS 1675. These initials refer to Richard and Barbara (née
Carlyon) Scobell.*

Harry Stark   E. J. Russell, St. Austell

John Stark and his wife, Fanny (née Oliver). Wearing typical farm-worker's clothes, John was photographed in the 1920's in the fields above the Count House at Menagwins Farm, where he worked for John Davey.

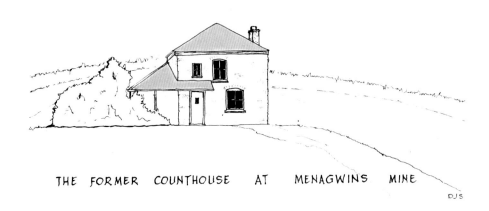

THE FORMER COUNTHOUSE AT MENAGWINS MINE

DJS

COUNTRY LIFE

I was brought up in an ordinary working-class family, as you might say, my father being employed as a farm cowman at Menagwins. Farmers who employed two men or more usually employed one as a cowman and the other would probably be a horseman. Sometimes, casual work would be carried out by hired labour for mangold and turnip hoeing, for hay and corn harvest, for threshing, and for the pulling of root crops. My family was poor in terms of money, but we never went short of food, and it was wholesome food at that. I remember my breakfasts of porridge, fried potatoes and fat bacon, or eggs if they were cheap. At dinner-time, we had plenty of vegetables as we grew our own, and we would have roast beef, rabbit or fowl pie, soup and broth with flatpole cabbage, and perhaps a figgy pudding afterwards. *(This, of course, was made of raisins, which the Cornish called 'figs'.)* What a feed you could have on a cold winter's day ! I particularly remember each of us having two pilchards and some boiled potatoes for tea on Monday nights. We also kept a pig to "salt in" for the winter, so we were never without salt pork and bacon. Many cottagers kept a pig to "salt in", and, in fact, some kept two - one for themselves and one to sell to the butcher, the money received being used to help pay the rent of their cottage. Pig-killing day was a busy day for the housewife. She had to boil gallons of water in the furnace, or boiler on the kitchen stove for use in removing the pig's bristles. Then came the "fry-up" next day with hinge pie, gurty-meat and hog's pudding. I was a butcher and can remember killing pigs at Trevarrick House, Methleigh House in Palace Road, Polcarne House, Penrice House and many others in the town and in the outlying villages.

Courtesy of The Francis Frith Collection

(Hinge pie was made from the liver, lungs and heart of an animal; gurty-meat was made of pigs' innards and groats; and hog's pudding was made of a pig's entrails stuffed with pork, breadcrumbs, herbs and spices.)

The way of farming in general has changed a lot. Cattle used to be housed in cattlehouses through the winter and were fed on barley, flatpole cabbages, mangolds and turnips. What a delight to step into a cattlehouse on a winter's day to be met by the warmth and smell of the cattle - except, of course, for their often foul-smelling breath !

The arrival of the threshing machine was an exciting occasion for us children, but not for the farmers' wives who had to prepare the beds and meals for the threshing machine men who lodged at the farms. These ladies would also prepare a score or more of pasties. Gateways were nearly always too narrow to allow the threshing machine easy access, and this necessitated men throwing down battens to keep the machine off the gateposts and to improve the line of approach. Sometimes, it could take a whole evening to get the machine into the yard when there were several gates along the route. I was always kept home from school on threshing day to rake the "doust", which was the dusty and dirty job usually reserved for boys. *(Doust is the chaff or husks of the corn.)*

Ploughs were drawn by horses, not tractors, and harvesting the corn was carried out with horse-drawn reaper-binders. The sheaves of corn which the binder produced were then stacked in the field, usually in shocks of seven sheaves, to enable them to dry out prior to being collected by wagons and taken to the mowhays and built into ricks or mows. Hay was cut by a horse-drawn reaper and after a few days of hot sunshine or drying wind the loose hay was collected and formed into ricks, which were then thatched with straw. Some mowing of hay was also done with scythes, and I have worked alongside five other men cutting hay in this way. The corn and hay harvests were often a chance for us boys to earn a little extra pocket money, and we were crafty enough to go to the farmers who paid us most and fed us with a nice supper afterwards! Paring of all hedges was carried out by hand-hook.

I have watched the timber men loading their wagons differently from the clay, cask and farm wagons. The horses got to know how much effort they must exert to get a tree trunk onto the wagon and when to stop so that they did not pull it off again. It was nice to see animal and man work together.

I used to help drive cattle from Tregorrick to Menabilly, near Fowey, for summer grazing, and also from Tregorrick via Duporth and Charlestown to Crinnis, over the old rough road there, with mine workings on one side and fields on the other. There were no houses at Crinnis then, and Sea Road did not exist. Incidentally, the house at Carlyon Bay Golf Course which later became the Clubhouse, was once the boyhood home of my father. My grandfather worked as an engine driver at the Wheal Eliza Mine at Tregrehan and I have heard my father say that he used to take him pasties regularly from their home at Crinnis for his midday meals.

Kathleen Rundell, Par

At the top of Brick Hill, Charlestown, the former lodge to Duporth House is shown here being in use as a Club for Duporth Holiday Camp which was established in 1934. Note the fancy fascias which were probably made of cast-iron, and also the arch over the entrance to the driveway.

Once the home of Charles Rashleigh, Duporth House was demolished in the late 1980's and some of the stone was taken to Antony House for use in its restoration.

Wm. Lyon, St. Austell

As children, we were often taken through Penrice Woods to Porthpean beach for a picnic, and I remember in those days that there would be hardly anyone on the beach. The Charlestown end of the beach was reserved for men and, consequently, one never saw any women in that area.

Porthpean

St. Austell Bay Hotel, Par, South Cornwall.
South and West view showing Club House and 18th green.

Within nine months of the laying of its foundation stone, when sheep were then grazing on the site, the St. Austell Bay Hotel was opened in April 1930 by the Earl of Mt. Edgcumbe. Designed by the architects, Messrs. Andrew & Randall of St. Austell, the 75-bedroom hotel was built by John Williams & Co. (Cornwall) Ltd., at a cost of £30,000. At Christmas 1931, a fire in one wing caused damage estimated at £15,000.

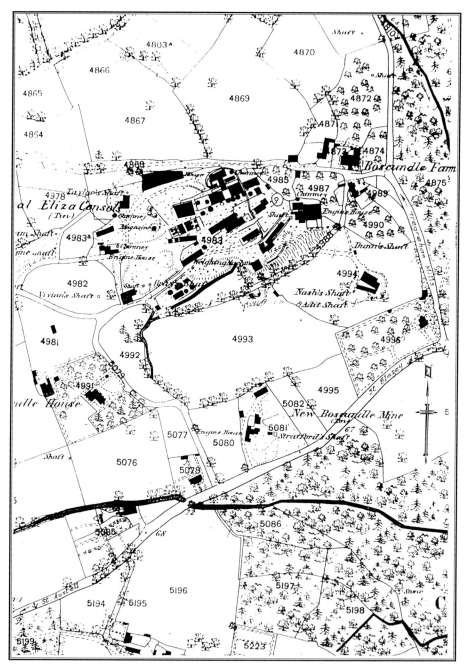

Reproduced from the 1881 Edition of the Ordnance Survey

9

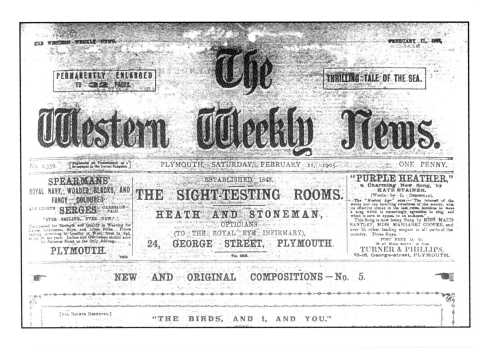

When I was a small boy, my father's wages were very low - somewhere around fifteen to eighteen shillings a week. A small part of this was spent on newspapers. We had, in our house, two weekly newspapers, The Western Weekly News from Plymouth and The St. Austell Star, both of which have now been discontinued. When I started school, I used to bring home the Daily News and the Daily Mirror as our first daily newspapers.

10

SCHOOLDAYS

My school days at West Hill were enjoyable. My teachers were Mr. Bird, "Daddy" Burns, Jim Golley who was killed in the First World War, and Messrs. Pearce, Climo, Hobba, Turner, Thomas, Lomer and Cloke. There were no school buses and no school meals. We had to carry a pasty or sandwich and the pasties were eaten cold. For a change, we were given a penny or two to go to the grocer's shop to buy broken biscuits from a large square tin. There were no wrapped packets then either. There was no central heating at school - just a round coal-fired stove. On rainy days, some of us who had to walk a long way got extremely wet, and we used to stand around the fire to dry our clothes. The Beckley boys and girls used to walk to school from Towan via Menagwins, a distance across fields and through lanes of approximately two and a half miles.

Mr. W. C. Bird who retired in 1920 after teaching for 38 years at St. Austell Central School.

When I first started in the infants school, I was given a slate on which to write with a slate pencil. I could never understand how they managed to get the slate pencils so round, but I remember well having to do my "A.B.C." with them.

We had no radio when I was a boy and, of course, no television ! Personally, despite all the criticism aimed at the media, I think these are two of the greatest inventions in my lifetime. My grandchildren will have seen and heard far more before they start their schooling than I did at the age of ten or eleven years. They may also learn to speak better English, but I think it would be sad if the Cornish dialect were to disappear. My brother, Ed, made one of the first "cat's whisker" wireless sets and neighbours used to visit our house at Tregorrick to listen to services broadcast on Sunday evenings.

It might be thought that, as children, we had little to amuse ourselves. How wrong ! It seems that today children only play games in the school playground. We, as boys, used to play football quite a lot; we had iron hoops with their iron guides for the winter; we played Rounders, Jump back, Nip-cross and with spinning tops, from which we pulled out the original spill and replaced it with a screw to help the top travel around in a large circuit. We also played marbles with Big Ring and Little Ring, Long Shot and Shot Coming In; Dog and Cat with a stick about two feet long, and another of six to eight inches *(a horizontal, overhanging shorter stick was struck vertically by the larger to propel it horizontally);* Duck Stone - an aiming game - which was played with fist-sized stones; Five Stones; Tig *(Tag)*; and Teek Whistle or Hollo *(Hollo is a Fox/Hare & Hounds type of game).* Then, of course, there was "conker-time", when the horse chestnut shed its large seeds.

This photograph was taken at St. Austell Central School, West Hill in 1905. My father is second from the right in the third row.

Back Row: (?); (?); Mabel Jenkins; Gladys Cornelius; B. Davies; (?); Maggie Chesterfield.

Fourth Row: - Pearce; Lena Grose; Gerrude Stephens; Clive Northcot; Louise Easterbrook; B. Blake; Ekla Edyvean; Mabel Norman.

Third Row: (?); -Welch; C. Allen; S. Kent; -Rosevear; F. George; T. Husband; (?); Harry Stark; (?).

Second Row: S. Kent; (?); (?); -Hocking; -Williams; -Williams; (?); Gerrude Panchion; (?); (?).

Front Row: (?); -Blake; (?); (?); -Tucker; (?); -Williams; (?).

12

The girls also had their games. They had large and small wooden hoops with sticks to hit them along, which was a good way to keep warm in winter. When small, they played at keeping shops and shopping; Mothers and Fathers; and make-believe cooking. The older girls played Hide and Seek; Skipping Ropes with Jump-In; and Hop-Scotch.

A lot of games used to be played in the roads as there was little traffic to bother us. Occasionally, we did a little "minching" (playing truant) from school, especially in the afternoons, and were caned by the master on our return to school the next day. Our plan was to go as far as Pondhu Bridge and into the allotment fields to play for a while, and then on to the apple orchards at Tregorrick where we took what fruit we needed and ate it in the woods. We then waited for the rest of the children to come out of school so as to arrive home at the proper time to stop Mother from knowing what we had done !

Harry's mother portrayed in this watercolour painting by a travelling artist at Tregorrick in the early 1890's. Originally two cottages, the property is now one dwelling known as "Nutshell Cottage".

Shopping in my early days was also a great deal different than it is today. My mother gave her order to Mr. Box, the grocer, for the month's groceries, which included a bushel of flour, brought in a trap, which was then put in a large wooden hutch before being used to bake her bread and cakes. In those days, the practice was for the grocer to give the children a bag of sweets on settlement of his bill. I remember Mother used to go to "Daddy" Goodman's shop for other items, where a very kind lady assistant, a Miss Rundle, gave us sweets. Bars of salt measuring approximately 18" x 9" x 9" could be bought from Gaved's coalstore. People used these to "salt-in" their pigs. *(Gaved's coalstore was sited where the present B & Q road-side carpark now is.)* Today, people's tastes have changed, and pigs are no longer fattened to look like barrels; they look like greyhounds to my eye, as people no longer need fat bacon to make lard. *(Advertisements in the Cornish Guardian in November 1906 and October 1908 give the following prices for provisions at Goodman's and Lipton's, respectively.*

Tea	*10 1/2d. per 1b*	*Best Lump Sugar*	*1 3/4. per 1b.*
New Currants	*2 3/4d. per 1b*	*Granulated Sugar*	*1 1/2d. per 1b.*
Cheese	*7d. per 1b*	*Coffee*	*1s. 6d. per 1b.*
Figs	*2 1/2d. per 1b*	*Butter*	*1s. 1d. per 1b.*
Lard	*12s. 9d. per pail*		

As can be seen from the price of lard, it was certainly worthwhile keeping one's own pig !)

Davidson Bros.

This postcard, sent in February 1911, shows the West End of St. Austell and "Daddy" Goodman's shop which my father remembered so vividly.

When I was a boy, butter was preserved in the summer for winter use by salting it and storing it in "stugs". *(Stugs are large salt-glazed pots.)* In the summer, butter was about one shilling a pound and rose to 1/6d. during the winter, which was a considerable price in those days. Eggs were also pickled and sold for about 1/2d. each. Fish was sold from jowters' carts at so many for a shilling. *(Jowter is a Cornish term for a travelling fish-hawker.)*

(I can remember my own mother making butter from the surplus cream from the cow we kept when I was a child - childlike, however, I preferred the butter which had been bought !)

MARKET DAY & THE MARKET HOUSE

On Fridays, the local farmers brought their produce - mainly, butter, eggs and poultry - into the town by horse and pony traps. Stabling could be found at such places as:-

Harris' Yard, East Hill
Hoskin's White Hart Yard
Menear's Hotel, Market Hill
The Stag Yard, Duke Street
Neal's Yard, Vicarage Hill
The General Wolfe, Bodmin Road
New Inn Yard, off Fore Street
Golden Lion Yard, Church Street.

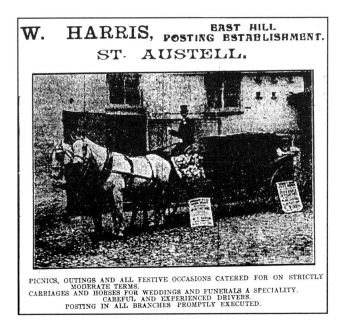

An advertisement which appeared in the Cornish Guardian in August 1913.

Most farmers rode into town on horseback. Some came in traps and errand-boys took the farmers' purchases back to the traps. In the days before motor-buses and cars, people could hire a horse carriage or trap. The station horse bus, driven by the White Hart's ostler, Billy Bone, took commercial travellers and their goods to the shops, as well as carrying people to and from the railway station. *(In January 1908, the St. Austell Station and Town Bus was newly managed by John W. Hoskin, proprietor of the White Hart Hotel.)*

15

This postcard sent from St. Ewe in 1908 invites Mrs. I. Kent of Pensagillas (a farm approximately 1¹/₂ miles north-west of St. Ewe village) to visit the sender. Note the horse-bus outside the White Hart Hotel.

On the main road to Mevagissey on the St. Austell side of Tregorrick, the treetops used to spread right over the road and there were no street lights after Gaved's Store near the present roundabout. It used to be awfully dark and muddy and, in addition, there was a ditch on one side of the road. I always had the fear that I might be knocked down by a farmer on horseback when it was really dark. I remember a fright I had one winter's night as I was making my way home. I was a boy of fourteen. Having left school, I had been working on a Friday in the Market House (6.15 a.m. to 9.30 p.m. - long hours then !), and when I left work it was wet and dreary, having rained most of the day. The level of the White River was high and the water could be heard roaring in the darkness. Suddenly, as I approached Mac Grose's house, I could hear chains rattling, and then in the darkness I saw something white. As I knew I was near Mac's house, I thought that nothing could go wrong, and I carried on walking towards my home. All of a sudden, Neddy Stephens' white pony flashed by with its chains dangling around its neck and rattling on the ground. The pony had broken out of its field. Wasn't I relieved to find it was not a ghost !

(Mac Grose lived in one of a group of cottages between the St. Austell & Pentewan Railway and the mica works at Trewhiddle, approximately on the site of the now-redundant E.C.C. laboratories. He was the yardman at the St. Austell railway terminus, and he was also in charge of the railway trucks as they ran by gravity from the terminus to Tregorrick in the days prior to 1908. After this date, the locomotives were permitted to cross the highway at Tregorrick.)

When I was a boy, old men talked about the Market House and its use as a home for many butchers' shops and other stalls. I can remember only a few of the butchers' shops that were there in my time:-

Bob Francis, St. Austell

Cole & George, Tregorrick

Kelly, Tregonissey

Richards, Stenalees

Yelland, Nanpean

Eggins, Mevagissey

Gammon, St. Austell.

16

There was also a butter market upstairs, where the women would put their large baskets on white tablecloths to display the goods. In summer, the butter was often covered with cabbage leaves to keep it cool. There were also two egg wholesalers, who packed their big wooden crates with straw to keep the eggs safe.

The Market House was also put to other uses. Flower Shows were held in it, with famous military bands playing there before giving concerts in the evenings at the Public Rooms in Truro Road.

(The 61st Annual Exhibition of the St. Austell Cottage Gardening Society was held in the Market House in July 1908. The Band of the Second Life Guards provided music during the day, and there was a grand promenade concert in the evening. The following year, it was the turn of H.M. Coldstream Guards to entertain. In 1910, the Royal Garrison Artillery Band was in attendance and the Market House was converted into a "veritable fairyland". Myriads of bannerettes were suspended from the roof, scores of massive flags hung on the walls, and the pillars were festooned with evergreens. The Cornish Guardian of 29th July in that year stated that the sombreness of the Market House had entirely disappeared, and in its stead were revealed all the beauties of nature - human as well as floral !)

O. F. (Stengel & Co. Ltd.)

In 1842, an Act of Parliament was given Royal Assent by Queen Victoria to allow the people of St. Austell to build a new market house and town hall. Built of local granite and having most impressive roof timbering, the building was opened in 1844. The rear of the building was once used as a Fire Station, whilst, at the front, the Town Hall was on the first floor.

Fat Cattle Shows were held in the Market House, and the Root Crop Show was held at the same time in the Town Hall. The Great Western Railway laid on cheap excursions in conjunction with the event.

(The first Christmas Fatstock Show was held in 1908, and a silver cup, donated by the Hon. T.C. Agar Robartes, was awarded to the owner of the champion beast. The St. Austell Orchestral Band was in attendance; admission was 1s. before 2 p.m. and 6d. thereafter, and dinners were available at the Queen's Head Hotel at 1 p.m. The Polienta Company was responsible for disinfecting the Market House at the conclusion of the Show!

There were butter-making competitions at the Fatstock Show which were open to students in the St. Austell district of the County Dairy School. This section of the Dairy School opened on 16th November, 1908 at Moor Cottage, Tregorrick, with twenty-two adult students in attendance.)

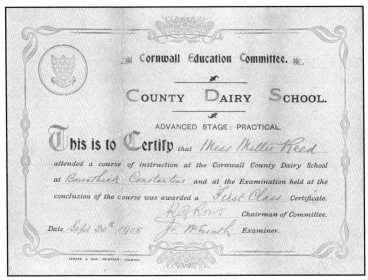

An example of the certificates that were awarded to successful pupils of the various branches of the County Dairy School.

At Christmas, the stalls in the Market House were colourfully decorated with large dressed dolls, especially Emmie Cundy's sweet stall. One of the most popular items to be sold was home-made rock. Just inside the main gate, Tommy Birchall had one of St. Austell's first chip stalls.

In my younger days, one could be entertained outside the Market House on Friday afternoons. Being Market Day, quack doctors, sword swallowers, and rope and chain escapologists came to the town. On Saturday evenings, the Salvation Army Band played outside before marching through Fore Street to the West End. In the summer, Mr. Staffieri sold ice-cream from his cart, and in the winter he sold hot roasted chestnuts.

During the Second World War, the Market House was used as a supply and delivery base for the area.

There used to be a big beam scale at the bottom of the steps inside the Market House which the butchers used. Hides were placed inside the bottom gates to be collected by the Grampound tanners. There was a little room near the butchers' stalls, where you could buy a steak or chop and have it cooked on the premises. Hot broth was also available.

BENNETT'S TANNERY
(From Old Photo)

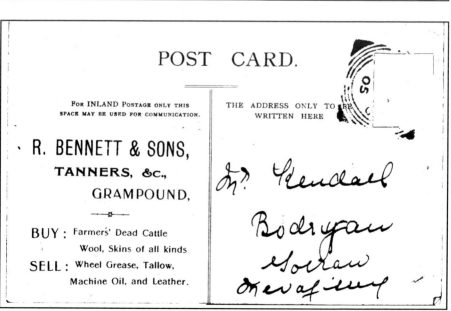

POST CARD.

For INLAND POSTAGE ONLY THIS SPACE MAY BE USED FOR COMMUNICATION.

THE ADDRESS ONLY TO BE WRITTEN HERE

R. BENNETT & SONS,

TANNERS, &c.,

GRAMPOUND,

BUY : Farmers' Dead Cattle
Wool, Skins of all kinds.

SELL : Wheel Grease, Tallow,
Machine Oil, and Leather.

SHOPS

I list below some of the shops and shop-keepers I recall as being in the town in my early and middle years.

HIGH CROSS STREET
- Coath (Photographer)
- Lyon's (Stationers)
- Rate Office (Mr. Bettison)
- Watkins (Auctioneer)

W.C. Lyon, St. Austell

The Post Office shown on the left was opened in May 1922 by Mr. James Perry, Chairman of St. Austell Urban District Council. Accompanied by Mr. Herbert Rowse, a Member of the Council, Mr. G.B. Dobell, Clerk, and Mr. E.D. Groves, Surveyor, Mr. Perry purchased the first stamp and despatched a telegram of congratulation to the Postmaster General. The postmaster was then Mr. Miles.

EAST HILL
- Moseley (Grocer)
- Post Office
- Stocker (Saddler)
- Thomas (Confectioner)
- Worthingon (Outfitter)

Kingsway (W. H. Smith)

Harris' posting establishment and Moseley's premises can be seen on the right-hand side of this photograph.

Derry Chapman, St. Austell

Worthington's shop and the General Post Office, when it was situated in East Hill, are visible through the floral arch built in the Bull Ring in 1909 to celebrate the visit of the Prince and Princess of Wales. In order to obtain a good view of the Royal couple, school-children were assembled in the Churchyard.

HOTEL ROAD	-	Comley (Watchmaker)
(that length of the	-	Fardon (a Quaker) (Draper)
present South St.	-	Kellaway (Saddler)
which extended	-	Lawry (Dairy)
from East Hill		
to Duke Street)		

CHURCH STREET	-	Box (Draper)
	-	Box (Grocer)
	-	Coon (Outfitter)
	-	Corn Exchange
	-	Reed (Jeweller)
	-	Stocker (Ironmonger)
	-	Truscott (Boot Shop)

Derry Chapman, St. Austell

This photograph taken from the Churchyard shows the junction of Church Street and Fore Street.
Masters' chemist shop in Fore Street can be seen in the centre of the picture.

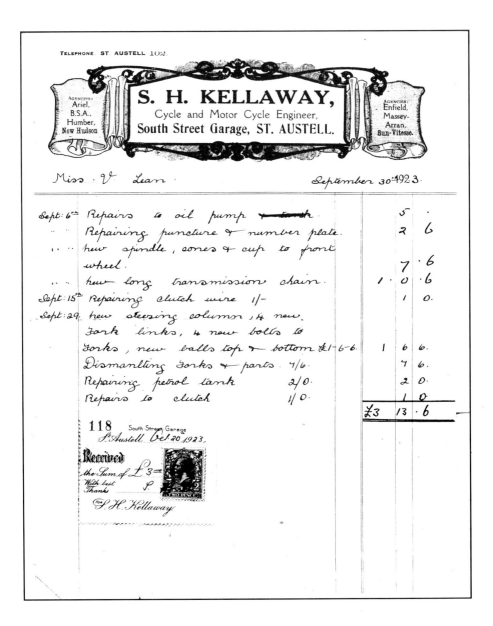

TELEPHONE ST. AUSTELL 102.

S. H. KELLAWAY,
Cycle and Motor Cycle Engineer,
South Street Garage, ST. AUSTELL.

AGENCIES:
Ariel,
B.S.A.,
Humber,
New Hudson

AGENCIES:
Enfield,
Massey-
Arran,
Sun-Vitesse.

Miss V Lean   September 30th 1923.

Date	Description		£	s	d
Sept 6th	Repairs to oil pump ~~tank~~			5	.
"	Repairing puncture & number plate.			2	6
"	new spindle, cones & cup to front wheel.			7	. 6
"	new long transmission chain.		1	0	. 6
Sept 15th	Repairing clutch wire 1/-			1	0.
Sept 29	new steering column, 4 new. Fork links, 4 new bolts to Forks, new balls top & bottom £1-6-6.		1	6	6.
	Dismantling Forks & parts. 7/6.			7	6.
	Repairing petrol tank 2/0.			2	0.
	Repairs to clutch 1/0.			1	0
			£3	13	. 6

118   South Street Garage
St Austell, Oct. 20. 1923.

Received
the Sum of £3 =
With best
Thanks   p.
For S. H. Kellaway

Two views of Church Street, showing (above) the location of the shops of the Box family and (below) F.E. Stocker. The 'Red Bank', designed by Silvanus Trevail, fronts the Bull Ring in the upper photograph which was taken in 1898.

Truscott's Central Boot & Shoe Store on the corner of Church Street and Fore Street stood next to Reed, the jeweller and optician. Pascoe's outfitters can be seen at the end of Victoria Place.

VICTORIA PLACE   -   Collins (Saddler)
                 -   Cross (Chemist)
                 -   Dawe (Draper)
                 -   Julyan (Paper Shop)
                 -   Nottle (Grocer)
                 -   Parnell (Hairdresser)
                 -   Pascoe (Outfitter)

DUKE STREET   -   Daniel & Rowse (Plumbers)
                 -   Lean (Fruiterer)
                 -   Lovering (Plumber)
                 -   Martin (Boot Mender)
                 -   Paul, Martin (Draper)
                 -   Russell (Photographer)
                 -   Staffieri (Chip Shop)
                 -   Telephone Exchange

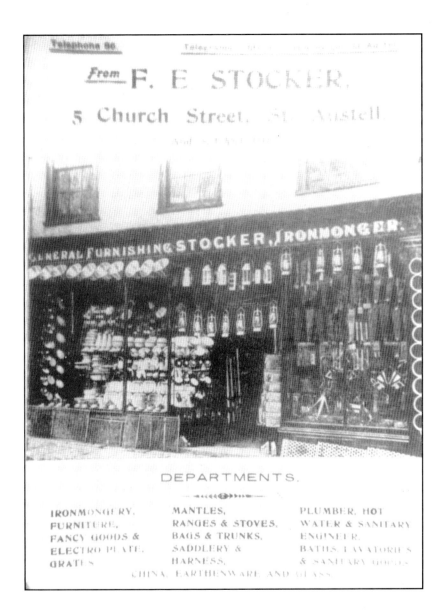

Telephone 80.   Telegrams: ... St Austell

From F. E. STOCKER,

5 Church Street, St. Austell

GENERAL FURNISHING STOCKER, IRONMONGER.

DEPARTMENTS.

IRONMONGERY,	MANTLES,	PLUMBER, HOT
FURNITURE,	RANGES & STOVES,	WATER & SANITARY
FANCY GOODS &	BAGS & TRUNKS,	ENGINEER,
ELECTRO PLATE,	SADDLERY &	BATHS, LAVATORIES
GRATES	HARNESS,	& SANITARY GOODS

CHINA, EARTHENWARE AND GLASS

MARKET STREET	-	Coombe (Hairdresser)
	-	Cook & George (Dressmaker)
	-	Eastman (Butcher)
	-	Rosevear (Draper)
	-	Warne, Sammy (Wallpaper & Toys)

On the right-hand side of this photograph taken in 1920, Frank Rosevear's drapers shop can be seen next to the Queen's Head public house. Hodge's name appears above that of Mann, the ironmongers, at the top of Vicarage Hill.

| TREGONISSEY ROAD | - | Hocking (Book Binder) |
| | - | Nicholls (Baker) |

| CROSS LANE | - | Thompson (Glazier) |

MENACUDDLE STREET	-	Co-op (Old Manor House)
(now North Street)	-	Griffin (Grocer)
	-	Smith (Decorator)

| VICARAGE HILL | - | Huddy (Barber) |
| | | (Cut boys' hair for 1d.) |

WEST HILL	-	Ivey (General Shop)
	-	Jenkin (Basket Maker)
	-	Pugh (Baker)
	-	Thomas (Grocer)
	-	Walters (Chip Shop and
		Secondhand Shop
	-	Williams (Grocer)

Harry Stark

FORE STREET	-	Bennett (Cloam Shop)
	-	Bennett (Shoe Shop)
	-	Bennetto, Mary (Tailor)
	-	Best (Drapers)
	-	Bice (Chemist)
	-	Blight (Outfitter)
	-	Broads (Drapers)
	-	Buzza (Butcher)
	-	Chesterfield (Fruiterer)
	-	Cole (Restaurant)
	-	Dunn (Seedsman)
	-	Ede (Papershop)
	-	Goodman (Grocers)
	-	Grose (Boot Shop)
	-	Grose (Draper)
	-	Hall, Evan J. (Draper)
	-	Hart (Butcher)
	-	Hawke (Ironmongers)
	-	Hawkins (Draper)
	-	Hemmings (Baby Shop)
	-	Hepworths (Outfitters)
	-	Hodge (Ironmongers)
	-	Hodge (Seedsman)
	-	Home & Colonial (Grocers)
	-	Huddy & Kneebone (Jewellers)
	-	Jacob (Cabinet Maker)

The west end of Fore Street with Tidy, the tobacconists, at the junction of Truro Road and Bodmin Road, next to Warne, the printers. West End Post Office at this time was kept by Mr. Reed and was situated next to Best & Son.

This postcard, postmarked May 1919 but photographed in 1912, shows the eastern end of Fore Street. The house projecting into the street behind the two ladies pushing perambulators was the dower-house of the Tremayne family of Heligan.

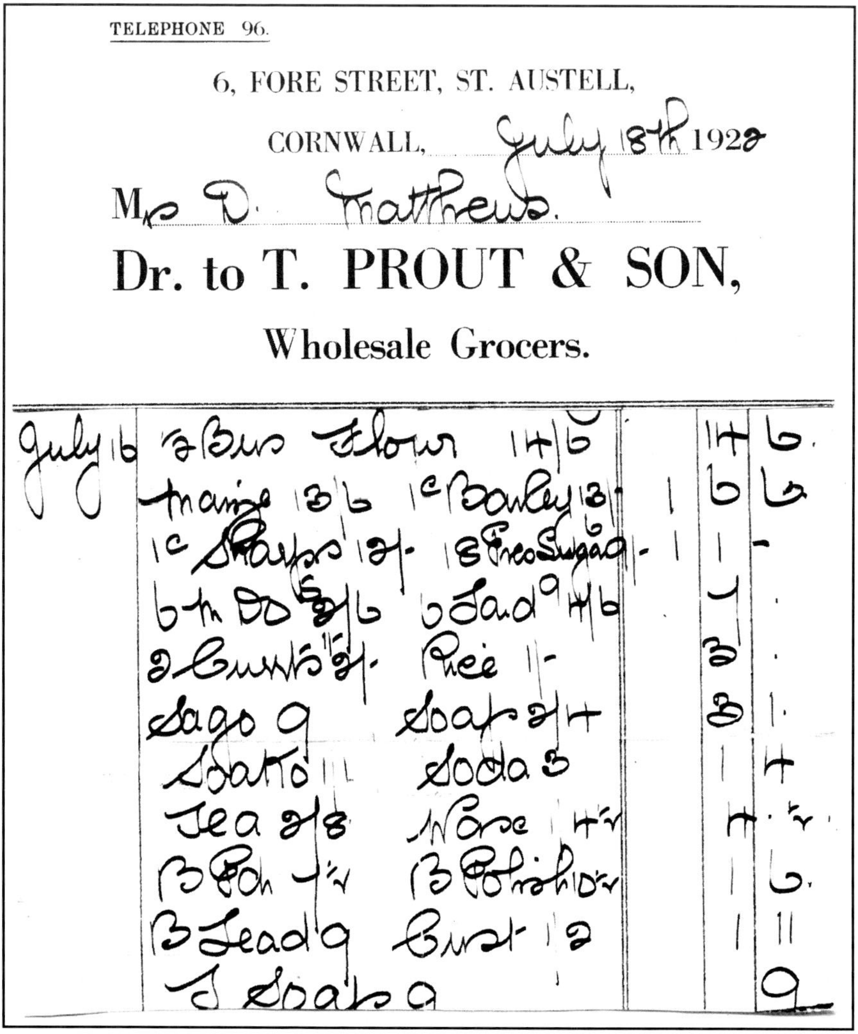

TELEPHONE 96.

6, FORE STREET, ST. AUSTELL,

CORNWALL, *July 18th* 192~~8~~

M*rs* D. *Matthews.*

Dr. to T. PROUT & SON,

Wholesale Grocers.

July 16	3 Bus Flour 14/6		14	6	
	Maize 13/6 1c Barley 13/-	1	6	6	
	1c Sharps 12/- 18 Preo Sugar	1	1	-	
	6th DD 5/6 6 Sand 4/6		5	-	
	2 Currts 3/- Rice 1/-	3			
	Sago 9 Soap 2/4	3	1		
	Salt 1 Soda 5	1	4		
	Tea 2/8 Nore 4/-	4			
	B Peal 1/- B Polish 1/-	1	6		
	B Lead 9 Curst 1/2	1	11		
	2 Soap 2			9	

David Juleff & Co. were situated on the corner of Fore Street and Menacuddle Street. In 1907, their 'Boun-tu-fit' suits could be purchased from 21/- to £4. In the large suite of rooms above the shop, a Social Club for the people of St. Austell was being established in 1909.

- Oliver (Boot Shop)
- Phillips (Draper)
- Phillips (Outfitter)
- Prout (Grocer)
- Real (Cabinet Maker)
- Reed (Post Office & Restaurant)
- Rogers (Grocer)
- Starsta (Grocer)
- Tregonning (Barber)
- Uglow (Music Shop)
- Varcoe (Bicycles)
- Vickery & Co. (Outfitters)
- Warmington (Tobacconist)
- Whetter (Jewellers)
- Whetter (Outfitter)
- Williams (Butcher)

JAMES McTURK & SON,
Central Restaurant and Temperance Hotel,
28, FORE STREET, ST. AUSTELL.

WILLIAM REAL,

Cabinet Maker
and
Upholsterer.

Undertaker.

FORE STREET,
ST. AUSTELL.

Telegrams:
'Real, Undertaker,
St. Austell.'

This shop was damaged in 1908, when one of Giles' wagons, laden with staves for a local cooperage, swayed and its contents collided with the shop front.

The timber planks lying in the carriageway at the junction of Fore Street and Church Street are here in the process of being made into a dais to greet the Prince and Princess of Wales on 10th June, 1909. Owners of houses overlooking the platform had a rich harvest from people who paid between half a guinea and 2 guineas to view the reception.

33

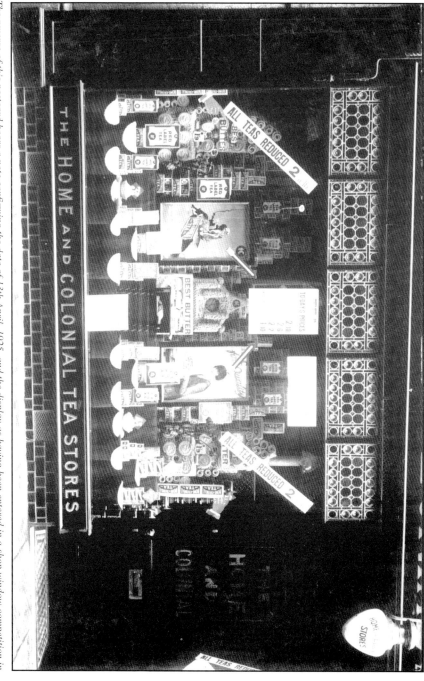

The reverse of this postcard bears a note confirming the date of 13th April, 1925, and the display as having been entered in a shop window competition in St. Austell.

Harry Stark

Children dancing the Flora in Truro Road. Almost far left, the roof of the three-storey property of Treloar's boot shop can be seen towering above the adjacent properties of Strike, the granite quoins of Doney, Son, Watts & Co., the arched facade of the Savoy Theatre, and also Hugo's shop. The Savoy - originally, St. Austell Picture Theatre Ltd. - opened on 13th October 1913, with seating for 380 people. It was owned by Mr. Ellis Slack, managed by a Mr. Corrison, and the pianist was Miss Isobel Jewell. Competition from the Odeon Cinema, which opened in 1936, would have been a contributory factor in its closure.

TRURO ROAD	-	Borlase (Chip Shop)
	-	Cook (Saddler)
	-	Doney (Monumental Mason)
	-	Hugo (Dairyman & Butcher)
	-	Pascoe (Barber)
	-	Strike (Draper)
	-	Strike (Outfitter)
	-	Tidy (Tobacconist)
	-	Treloar (Boot Shop)
	-	Truscott (Barber)
	-	Venner (Dairy)
	-	Warne (Printer)
BODMIN ROAD	-	Frost (Music Shop)
	-	Hancock (Grocer)
	-	Harvey (Cloam Shop)
	-	Pappin (Grocer)
	-	Warmington (Fruiterer)

SOUTH STREET	-	Giles (Builder)
	-	Glanfield (Baker)
	-	Kellaway (Garage)
	-	Staffieri (Ice Cream)

There was a quaint old chemist called Masters in Fore Street. He had an artificial leg, and he used to pull up his trouser leg in the shop and oil the leg when it squeaked. He had a mannerism that if you asked for a certain thing, he would say, "No, take this - it's cheaper and better."

At "Daddy" Goodman's shop, you could see bladders of lard hung up for sale, and at some grocers they used to put boxes of dried cod fish in the doorways. With dogs roaming around, you can just imagine what people thought and said !

Most of the young people of the town congregated in Fore Street on Saturday nights, and consequently it was crowded. The shops did not close until nine or ten o'clock, and at about eight o'clock Bobby Francis, the butcher, could be seen leading his pony and trap through the town on his way home after the rounds.

Harry Stark

Thomas Cook, the saddler, occupied premises in Truro Road, which are currently used by Blaylock's opticians. The large building in the centre, now accommodating The China Spot, and Adeba Nurseryworld, was once the town house or dower-house of the Sawle family of Penrice. Their crest and motto can still be seen above the first-floor windows .

FEAST DAYS

In my younger days, St. Austell Feast Week was held in early June, and the area was a hive of activity for three days from Monday to Wednesday. The wagoners started work very early in the morning to get time off later. The festivities began with Charlestown Regatta on the Monday.

Older people talk of "Eckey" Johns of Mevagissey, who once dived under the water for so long that a French captain dived in after him, only to find "Eckey" quite all right. My uncle, Bill Stark from Charlestown, was known as "The Greasy Pole Man".

(The Greasy Pole was a popular form of entertainment, in which a stout pole was cantilevered over the edge of a quay, and two contestants sitting on it each tried to knock the other into the harbour with a 'pillow'.)

Harry Stark

A well-attended Regatta Day at Pentewan. Crowds flocked to these popular events, and Pentewan held its first Regatta in July 1914. A greasy pole can be seen hanging over the dock basin outside the harbour office.

SAVED OVER THIRTY LIVES.

ADVENTUROUS LIFE OF ST. AUSTELL MASTER MARINER.

EXPERT DIVER.

A very familiar figure in the streets of St. Austell is Captain John Johns, who is very well-known and popular. He was born at Mevagissey 77 years ago and all his life has been spent seafaring.

He won the first prize at Charlestown for diving for five years in succession, and was never beaten. He has saved over thirty lives around Mevagissey, and has many medals, parchments, etc., as testimonies to his courage and ability. One silver medal of which he is very proud, was awarded by the R.S.P.C.A. for rescuing a cow from a well near Mevagissey.

About 25 years ago he dived six times in an endeavour to bring the body of a man to the surface of a clay pit at St. Dennis, the man having dropped to the bottom of a pool and his body was caught about 50 feet down.

One winter between 30 and 40 years ago Capt. Johns was sent for when the dock gates at Pentewan were jammed. With hammer and chisel in his hands he dived to the bottom and cut through a bolt and the trouble was overcome.

On one occasion in Rotterdam a ship's boiler which was being hauled on to a ship fell into the sea and sank, and Capt. Johns dived into 25 feet of water, fixed a sling on the sunken boiler, which was safely pulled to the surface.

A BLIZZARD MEMORY.

At the time of the great blizzard in 1891, Capt. Johns was captain of the schooner Sterling, of Fowey, from Antwerp to London, and only three boats of a considerable fleet returned home.

He once saved two boys who fell into Mevagissey harbour. One sank to the bottom, but Capt. Johns dived and recovered him, and after he had got him to the shore the other boy had sunk. Capt. Johns immediately dived and saved him.

When a big ship was being towed from Victoria Docks, London, to Cardiff, in 1883, a wire hawser fouled the propeller of the tug. Capt. Johns dived three times, and eventually freed the hawser.

When only 18, when Capt. Johns was one of the crew of the schooner John Pearce, of which his father was master, Capt. Johns, with three others, saved 14 marines and an officer who were in distress in a Revenue cutter in Cardiff Roads.

One of his very popular feats at Mevagissey regatta was to dive off the top of the parapet near the lighthouse at low water.

Off Mevagissey Bay once, a mackerel seine net became entangled with rocks, and Capt. Johns, fully clothed, dived in and cleared them. On that occasion he had to stay under water for two minutes.

Capt. Johns gave up bathing only two years ago, and the last exhibition he gave was at Newquay in 1914 when he dived off the tower into only three or four feet of water.

❖❖❖❖❖❖❖❖❖❖❖❖❖❖❖❖❖❖❖

An extract from The Royal Cornwall Gazette and Cornwall County News 6th December, 1933

38

Derry Chapman, St. Austell

Victoria Road, Mount Charles, with members of various Chapels and Sunday Schools marching behind their banners and local bands. This procession can be seen to extend at least halfway up Watering Hill (Alexandra Road).

E 34500 Union Road, S⁺ Austell.

O. F. (Stengel & Co. Ltd.)

Clifden Road was previously known as Union Road, reputedly because it formed a 'union' between different ecclesiastical parishes. In 1907, residents of Mount Charles were obtaining their drinking water supply from a stream by the side of Union Road or from "Cooks Shoot (sic)" at Polkyth.

JUNE 11, 1909.

MOUNT CHARLES FEAST.

—:o:—

SUNDAY SCHOOL DEMONSTRATION.

—:o:—

A BRILLIANT SPECTACLE.

—:o:—

In the sunlight of a perfect June day Mount Charles annual Feast was celebrated on Tuesday with feasting and merry making. The principal event of the day was the annual demonstration of the Sunday Schools in the Mount Charles district, and judging by the immense crowds of people that visited the locality this ever-popular event is certainly not diminishing in favour, but each succeeding year brings a larger number of visitors than before. The principal thoroughfares became, shortly after mid-day, the scene of considerable activity. Bands began to arrive, and children and teachers hurried to their respective schoolrooms to join in the procession. The principal business houses were closed, and altogether, with the lavish display of flags and bunting, the locality presented a holiday appearance.

The attraction of the afternoon was the parade of the Sunday School children. Never before in the history of Mount Charles has a more brilliant spectacle been witnessed. The Mount Charles Wesleyan and United Methodist Sunday Schools set off early by way of Watering Hill for King's Avenue, and after visiting the grounds of Mr. E. Carlyon, of Polkyth, returned to Union Road, where they met the Charlestown Wesleyans. The Primitive Methodists, adhering to the old route, paraded the town, after calling at Mr. Carlyon's. They were the first to arrive at Mount Charles, where they joined the Bethel United Methodists, who also took part in the march past. After the Wesleyans (2) and United Methodists had perambulated the neighbourhood of Ranelagh Road they, too, returned to Victoria Road on the way to their respective fields. To witness the march past thousands of people congregated at Victoria Road. Nearly 1,000 children took part in the demonstration, and the scene witnessed was a memorable one. It was a notable day for the children, and one of triumph and gratification for those who have an interest in Sunday School work. The bands in the procession were Mount Charles Independent (Charlestown Wesleyans), Queens (Mount Charles U.M.), St. Austell (Primitive Methodists), S. Stephens (Bethel United Methodists).

THE TEA TREATS.

When the parading was over, and the schools had dispersed, the real feast began. In fields lent for the occasion the children were regaled with tea and cakes, and for an hour teachers and officers were busily engaged supplying their wants. Public teas were provided for visitors by each school, and were very largely patronised. Mount Charles Wesleyans occupied a field at Porthpean Road, where the tables were served by the Misses G. and E. Bowden, M. Peters, E. Higman, N. and B. Ripper, M. and N. Truscott, M. and E. Clemes, Jenkin, E. Harper, and Mesdames W. H. Manning, M. Truscott, L. Truscott, and Houseman The United Methodists occupied their usual field, and received their share of patronage at the tea served by Mesdames S. Harper, Tregonning, Nancarrow, Phillips, Pascoe, Mewton, Moses, Harvey, Parnall, Tyzzer, Mably, and the Misses B. Tyzzer Mably, Harper, and Williams. The tea tables at the Primitive Methodists were superintended by Mesdames G. Rowe, T. Allen, H. Rowe, J. Rundle, J. Hammer, S. Rowe, Lenderyon, J. Stephens, S. Pearce, Minear. Misses A. Ennis, J. Stephens, E. Mitchell, H. Hearn, and A. Blewett.

EVENING FESTIVITIES.

The hours which followed were given up to general enjoyment. Bands discoursed lively airs and amusements were provided for the young. The centre of attraction was Messrs. Ware's roundabouts, which proved as popular as ever with old and young. Even up to a late hour people kept up the spirit of revelry with "teaser" and confetti, and it was not until nearly midnight that the remnant of a tired but good-natured crowd dispersed and quietness once more reigned at Mount Charles until another Feast Tuesday.

An extract from the Cornish Guardian 11th June, 1909

Tuesday was Mount Charles' "day". Schoolchildren from the Sunday Schools and, I think, from Charlestown used to march behind bands to meet at the Duke of Cornwall Inn, Mount Charles, and go to their various tea fields. They had their big kissing-ring games, and other games in the evening, and then visited a fun fair. The sweet stalls, or "stan'ings" as they were often called, would be erected by the side of the main road and up towards Union Road *(now Clifden Road)* to near the railway bridge. They were illuminated during darkness by naphtha lamps. Here, I can remember the travelling Italian ladies wearing colourful head scarves, and telling your fortune from cards selected by love-birds.

Wednesday was St. Austell's "day". There were tea treats, and horse sports were organised either at Rocky Park or Poltair Football Field. The sports events included horse jumping, flat racing, pony and donkey racing, pebble-picking with donkeys and cycle racing with visiting professionals from as far away as Plymouth. The day finished with a Flora dance through Fore Street. *(Prize money, in 1906 for example, for the donkey race ranged from 15s. to 5s., and for the donkey and trap race from £1 to 5s. In 1908, the results of the donkey race were 1st W. Nicholls, St. Austell; 2nd H. Gilbert, Stenalees; and 3rd Stark, London Apprentice - "Stark" was probably my father's grandfather, Tom, riding 'Cinderella', a donkey well known in the area. He was the only entrant for the second donkey race which he rode facing backwards and consequently was awarded the first prize !)*

Harry Stark

Horse racing at Rocky Park took place in fields on the brow of the hill between St. Austell and St. Mewan. The buildings of St. Austell Brewery are just visible on the skyline.

(Other events took place on Feast Wednesday. In 1907, the Band of D. Coy. D.C.L.I. (St. Austell) provided entertainment, and later Miss Maria Yelland - the popular Cornish mezzo-soprano, who had had considerable success in the London halls - took part in a Grand Concert in the Public Rooms.)

The village of Trethurgy held its Feast Day on the following Thursday.

MY VISIT TO TRETHURGY FEAST.

—:o:—

A HALF-DAY'S NOVEL EXPERIENCES.

—:o:—

(Special to this Paper))

—:o.—

Trethurgy Feast, sir?

Jump up, sir.

I nodded my head and took my seat in a brake in the Bull Ring. I had often heard of Trethurgey Feast, but never before Thursday did I have the opportunity of paying a visit to this annual rustic gathering, in one of the most remote corners of Mid-Cornwall. For years; in fact, ever since I began to wear long trousers and smoke a cigarette, I have made it a rule to see all the out-of-the-way curious and unique sights that come my way, and that curiosity, call it what you will, has led me into all manner of queer places, but never, I believe, have my eyes beheld such a delightful rustic event as Trethurgey Feast.

The brake was fast filling up when I took my seat in the corner, and in a minute or two when nineteen had taken the places of a dozen when the driver let go the drag, cracked his whip, and we were off.

Someone started "out on the ocean sailing," but singing soon gave way to chatter, and as we went rattling along many a merry jest flitted to and fro the conveyance. With one or two exceptions we were a jovial party. My right hand neighbour was a very precise individual indeed; I don't think he smiled once the whole of the way, but whenever he had a chance to make himself heard he grumbled either about the heat, the roads, or the Budget. He reminded me of an old tutor of mine who looked as serious as an undertaker, except on quarter-days. Not so the others. Except, of. course, the couple who sat opposite me, and they were demure enough, goodness knows. But it was excusable, for they were in love, and had got it badly. They talked at intervals in monosyllables, but I knew by the hand clasps—their arms were tightly linked— and the lovelight in the eyes of the young man that he was telling the old story and following in the footsteps of his father. But of the others the one I think I liked best was the old lady with the red roses in her 8¾d. hat. She was a trifle outspoken, but what did it matter, we were out for the day.

What there was about me more than the others to attract her particular attention I do not know, except it was that I was a stranger. Our conversation began, as every conversation does, about the weather and then she asked me the all-important question "Had I been to Trethurgey Feast before?" I replied in the negative, and then she treated me to a downright thorough descriptive story of everything there was to be seen.

Her friend, a faded, tired-looking little woman, with a noisy child on her knees, chimed in with "we always have a good tay up here." "High tea," I asked. "'igh," she replied, "'igh up and plenty of caake and crain."

"Yes, my dear," said the woman with the red roses, whose name was Mrs. Brown, "you get treated right well up Trethurgey. I know, for I haven't missed going for thirty year, I haven't."

"Of course, you are thinking of the girls," was her next remark, but though I hastened to assure her that such thoughts were far from me she shook her head, and entered on a long and not uninteresting description of the qualities, good, bad and indifferent, of the Trethurgey girls. So I sat and listened, and not a word could I get in edgeways while Mrs. Brown and her friend talked unceasingly of the merits and demerits of the designing mammas, the engaging wenches, Cornish cream and saffron cake to be found at Trethurgey Feast.

On alighting, we found ourselves in the thick of the festivities. The little village lane was simply alive with feasters. Quaint little canvas-covered stalls behind which were garrulous women and buxom maidens, displaying for sale every conceivable form of sweetmeat, from the humble yard of liquorice to the three-coloured stick of home-made rock.

In and among the crowd mingled an ever-increasing number of children, who spent their pence with alacrity, and the result of their purchases was a disquieting and nerve-racking fanfare of squeakers and paper trumpets. To me the Feast field was the most interesting sight of the day. Here had foregathered a multitude from everywhere. We were, as it happened, just in time for the "feast." So with the others of the party I

sat down at one of the tables, and for half an hour consulted the world-famous Cornish cream and saffron cake. One has often heard of the hearty Cornish hospitality, and if the sort meted out at Trethurgey is anything of a sample the description has not been glorified one little bit.

Truly I thought this is the land of milk and honey. One really could not eat enough to satisfy the good old soul, resplendent in a new terra cotta blouse, that presided at our table, and ever and anon inquired "Be 'e making a good tay, Tom," or "'ave 'nother piece of cake, Bill?"

Up and down the Feast field there was endless frivolity and amusement. The old and middle-aged folks for the most part contented themselves with lazily sitting in the shade and finding sufficient enjoyment in watching the others. But it was the young people I was most interested in. Queens of the Feast there were by the score, and the young gallants were no less in number, for almost every Angelina had her Edward. In one corner of the field a game of kissing-in-the-ring was in progress, and, evading the watchful eye of my friend with the red roses, I gradually drew nearer. How it happened I don't in the least know, but just as I had taken my place in the ring the soft velvety arms of a girl were entwined around my collar, and her rosy lips had touched mine. For a shy individual like me this was unbearable, and I stole stealthily away—but not before I had paid the toll—to another part of the field. In a minute I was "tigged," and when I politely asked the fair creature who had condescended to touch the sleeve of my coat what it all meant, she laughingly replied "You tig me; come on," and, of course, I went.

When I got near to where Mrs. Brown was sitting, I was asked in the broad but musical tones of a village girl if I would "give anything for the band." Of course, I was not buying a brass band that afternoon, so I told her I had no use for such a thing, but when she said "Wont'ee gimme something fur 'em playing?" I was fairly caught, and had to hand over a "siller."

What to do with myself for the rest of the evening I did not know. I had tried a shot at the clay pipes, and knocked at the door of "Eliza" to find her safely at home. I had tried to win 5s. for 2d., and failed, and I had had a taste of the games, but now I was "up against it," as the Americans say. Suddenly, however, I noticed a fair native of the village, and Mrs. Brown not being within reach I strolled leisurely forward and raising my hat with a fetching "How-do-you-do? Pleased-to-meet-you, don't-you-know," kind of greeting, we were soon in conversation. My experiences for the next hour must be for ever a sealed book. Suffice it to say my companion took me to see the famous "Curngrey" Rock, the old farmyard pump, the ducks in the pool, and the village chapel. Of course, I expressed my unbounded delight at having met her and thanked her, perhaps too profusely, for comforting me in my loneliness. "Comforts," she said, "why you haven't given me any yet," and then she told me that to do the thing properly I should have to buy her half a pound of "comforts" at the "standin'," and so when we returned to the field I did her bidding and she treated me to a ginger-bread.

By this time night was swiftly advancing, and the "snail creep" was in its last stages. Tete-a-tetes were in full swing, and here and there tired out paterfamilias and youngsters were gathering up their belonging and getting ready to go home.

Into the brake a few minutes later I scrambled, and once more came under the critical gaze of Mrs. Brown. There was not much opportunity for conversation, for as we drove back to St. Austell "Lead kindly light," "We won't be home till morning," and "Roll the ball along," followed each other in quick succession to be repeated over and over again.

"Where's my 'feasting' young man?" Mrs. Brown asked me between the hymns, and when I told her that I was quite ignorant of what she meant she seemed quite put out, and made pointed reference to kissing ring adventures, which I, of course, resented. But when we pulled up in the Bull Ring she took me by the arm and whispered coaxingly "Come to tea next Sunday, will 'ee, my dear," and I promised her I would.

An extract from the Cornish Guardian 25th June, 1909

43

ENTERTAINMENT

My first entertainment as a small boy was the Concert and Coffee Supper, as it was called, which was held in the Church schoolroom in South Street - the long single-storey building opposite the entrance to Duke Street. Admission was 3d., which included a cup of coffee at the end. Actually, we never paid because we used to carry in the milk which was given by Mr. Johnnie Williams of Tregorrick ! Entertainment took the form of solos, comic songs, sketches, limericks, memory competitions and games.

On Saturday afternoons, we used to go to the Picturedrome in the Town Hall. For a week's duration in the Public Rooms in Truro Road, we also had Poole's Myriorama, which was a fine show in those days. We had travelling stage shows at times, and also musical comedies and plays.

(The Picturedrome was at one time run by Mr. Norman Gilberte. He was a former manager of the Savoy, and was one of the earliest producers of Gilbert & Sullivan operas in the town.

Poole's Myriorama was advertising itself in 1906 as having been "seventy years before the public". The show visited St. Austell annually in the autumn and it drew large audiences at the Public Rooms. Each picture show included historical events, such as the Battle of Trafalgar or the Advance and Defeat of the Spanish Armada, and topical or educational presentations such as the Destruction of San Francisco by an Earthquake, Lieutenant Shackleton's Dash for the South Pole, or the Loss of the Titanic. The programme was supplemented usually by a soloist or group of singers, performing animals (dogs or birds) and an acrobat, ventriloquist or magician. Poole's Myriorama was accompanied by its own orchestra.)

A. Hicks' series

The Fair Park in Gover Road with one of Birchall's showman's wagons in the centre of the picture. A company was to be formed by St. Austell Mercantile Association to equip this site for use as a cattle market in 1907. After sixty people had each invested £5, the Market Commissioners were to manage the enterprise under the Markets Act.

In the fair park at the bottom of Truro Road, there was a small wooden theatre in which plays were performed. Sometimes, a circus visited St. Austell and, in my young days, it processed through the streets. This was very colourful. In addition, we had Anderton and Rowlands' Gondolas; Hancock and Sister Sophie with galloping horses; Bostock and Wombwell's Menagerie; Bostock's Circus, and various other entertainments.

(The arrival of Bostock and Wombwell's Menagerie - a long convey of about twenty wagons drawn by sixty horses - would have been an amazing sight and, no doubt, caused much excitement.

Traction engines were also used, the two most famous being named 'Rajah' (Burrell No. 3509, built in 1913) and 'Nero' (Burrell No. 3669, built in 1915). The impressive 'Rajah' is owned by Clive and Marion Gibbard, and is exhibited at Dingles' Steam Village, Milford, Lifton, Devon, where Clive is the museum's engineer.)

Miss AURORA'S EQUESTRIAN LION "D'ARTAGNAN"

COL. T. TALLON'S LEONINE PUPILS.

MONS. VICTOR BATTY'S URSINE PUPILS

An extract from the Cornish Guardian 16th July, 1909

An extract from the Cornish Guardian 5th May, 1911

SKETCHES AT BOSTOCK AND WOMBWELL'S

TWISTING IT DOWN

THE WOMBAT

THE ELEPHANT ANOINTS HIMSELF WITH HIS BEDDING.

TASMANIAN DEVIL

AN AUSTRALIAN

CAPT WOMBWELL AND HIS PET LION

"JEROME" THE GREAT MANDRILL

FEEDING TIME

We would draw our readers' attention to the visit to Bodmin, on Thursday, July 22nd, of the Royal Show. It is some years now since their last visit. Since then the show has added very extensively numerous additions of novelties and unique animals never before seen in a travelling menagerie.

A visit to this famous show of a couple of hours and one learns more of the habits of the denizens of the forests of tropical countries than a year's book-learning. The great est boon to children to open their minds to the great Creator's works—a lesson they will never forget.

The numerous carriages will contain amongst other unique specimens of forest and jungle habitues the finest and largest lions in Europe to-day — tigers, leopards, bears, hyenas, wolves, jaguars, a waggon load of monkeys, beautiful aviaries of for eign birds, all the latest novelties in the animal world, including a white kangaroo carrying young. Tasmanian devils, the smallest horse alive. Wild boars from Wind sor Great Park, presented to Mr. E. H. Bostock by his Majesty the King as a mark of esteem.

There are three famous world-renowned lion tamers with this mammoth collection, who give daring performances at intervals with all classes of wild animals. There are herds of elephants, camels, and dromedaries for the children to ride on.

A splendid military band will play all the latest selections up-to-date at each perform ance.

In coming once more to Bodmin we wish the proprietors all the success they deserve.

Will also visit Liskeard, July 21st; Lost withiel, July 23rd; St. Austell, July 24th.

AFTER THE PAINTING OF G. SOURY, PARIS.

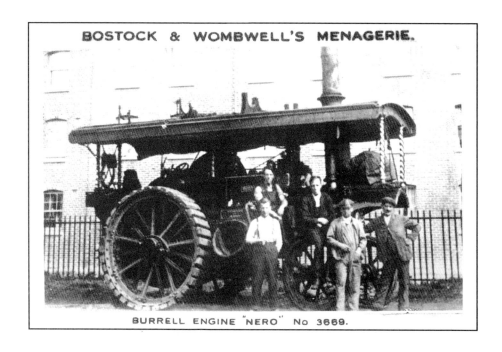

BURRELL ENGINE "NERO" No 3669.

Derry Chapman, Mount Charles, St. Austell

This photograph by Derry Chapman of Mount Charles contains all the instruments associated with a Fife and Drum Band. He being the nearest photographer to Porthpean, it is most likely that the band is the Porthpean Fife & Drum Band, photographed at the junction of Ranelagh Road and Union Road.

I have been told that some of the young men from Tregorrick used a lane (Field Lane) and pathway through a field to get to Porthpean to play in the Porthpean Fife and Drum Band. *(Bands of this type consisted of fifes (small flutes in B Flat), other larger and smaller flutes, side drums, base drum, cymbal and triangle.)*

On Easter Monday, horse shows, which included horse-driving classes, were held in the football field off Tregonissey Road *(now Trevarthian Road)*, to which the Great Western Railway ran special cheap-fare trains.

H. Gibbs, St. Austell

This postcard was posted in July 1910 to Miss G. Slade of Fowey and the sender states that he was camping in the same tent as last year at Mr. Stephens' farm.

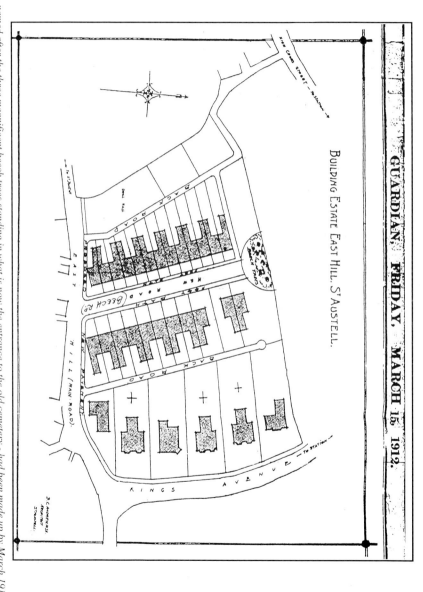

GUARDIAN, FRIDAY, MARCH 15, 1912.

BUILDING ESTATE EAST HILL, S^T AUSTELL.

Beech Road - named after the three magnificent beech trees standing in what is now the entrance to the old cemetery - had been made up by March 1912 and plots were ready for building operations to begin. The prices of the plots fronting Beech Road varied between £35 and £70 whilst those facing Kings Avenue ranged from £93 to £205.

50

I can remember a Flower Show being held in fields which are now the area of Beech Road, and also a show in Pondhu House fields near the mill.

When my friends and I acquired bicycles, we went to the dances at Pentewan. The red oil lamps on the bicycles often blew out on rough nights. The police used to meet at night at the old blacksmith's shop at London Apprentice - one from Mevagissey, one from Sticker and one from St. Austell. Woe betide you if you were caught riding a bicycle without a light ! *(In November 1908, the Cornish Guardian carried a report of someone being fined 6d. plus costs for riding a bicycle with no lights. A similar offence at St. Dennis merited a fine of 2s. 6d. !)*

The former London Apprentice Inn (the original smaller inn was incorporated in this building) and the building opposite, which once accommodated the village's blacksmith's shop. Historians, Hitchins & Drew, recorded that in the early part of the 19th century, the Sexton would go to St. Austell Parish Church on Easter Sunday wearing a cocked hat, and, after the service, he would announce in the Churchyard that the hat was "to be wrestled for tomorrow afternoon at London Apprentice". The inn, and subsequently the village, possibly took its name from a once-popular ballad entitled "The Honour of an Apprentice in London."

I can also recall King George V's Coronation Day in 1911. The villagers of Tregorrick, London Apprentice and Little Polgooth joined together and held their festivities and a united service on the lawn of Moor Cottage, a substantial private residence near Trewhiddle House. Children received medals and participated in sports in the evening before giving a concert during which they sang patriotic songs.

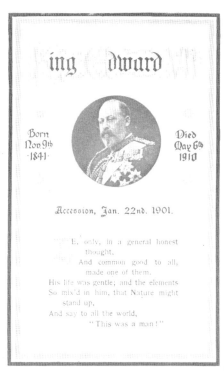

C. W. Faulkner & Co. Ltd.

(Raphael Tuck & Sons) Fine Art Developments Plc.

This multiple-view postcard depicts various aspects of the house and grounds at Moor Cottage (also known as the White House), near Tregorrick. Owned by the Coode family, the house was once tenanted by the Smith family, who ran it as a guest-house for many years.

The "White House," St Austell, Cornwall.

The first aeroplane I saw was at Rocky Park and it was flown by the Frenchman, Monsieur Salmet.

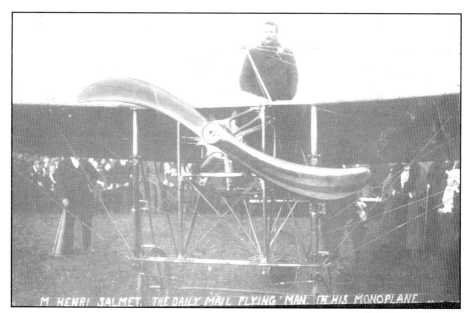

E. A. Bragg, Falmouth

Flying Man at St. Austell.

FINE EXHIBITION.

WELCOMED BY HUGE CROWDS.

An infectious wave of excitement swept over St. Austell on Tuesday afternoon when M. Salmet, the daring little Frenchman, who is touring the West-country, under the auspices of the "Daily Mail," made his long-anticipated flight to St. Austell.

The original intention was that the airman should fly from Falmouth to Fowey and St. Austell on Saturday, but the weather proved so unfavourable that his flight had to be postponed. On Saturday evening a town's meeting was called by Mr. James Perry, J.P. (chairman of the Urban Council), who, on account of the death of his father, was unable to be present. A committee was formed, of which Mr. A. E. Gaved was appointed hon. secretary, it being decided to charge 6d. entrance fee to the Rocky Park, kindly lent by the Golf Club, as the alighting place, and to present M. Salmet with £10, the balance after payment of expenses to go to the Cottage Hospital and Nursing Association. Arrangements were made for the reception of the airman on Monday evening, when he was expected to arrive and for exhibition flights on Tuesday, all being subject, of course, to "weather permitting."

On Monday evening a large crowd and vehicles of all kinds assembled on the road adjoining the Rocky Park, and in the field itself in expectation of seeing the flight, but the weather deterred the carrying out the programme. The next message was that he would arrive at six the next morning (Tuesday), and again a large crowd gathered, and were again disappointed. Two o'clock was the next time announced for his arrival, and from that time throughout the afternoon a large crowd waited patiently with hope deferred from hour to hour. At last at about 5.20 a speck was seen on the horizon in the direction of Falmouth, which, becoming larger, sent the watching crowds into rapturous excitement, as for the first time they saw the thrilling spectacle of an airman in flight. It was a great moment. The crowds were too spellbound to speak as they watched the aeroplane glide over the town in the direction of Fowey.

The news quickly spread that the airman would be returning to St. Austell flying ground shortly. About an hour later a buzzing sound heralded the re-appearance of the machine, which, travelling swiftly, made a graceful descent upon the Rocky Park. By this time an immense crowd had gathered in the field and along the roads and fields adjoining; motor cars, carriages, motor cycles, cycles, baby carriages, and every other form of locomotion occupied the thoroughfares, while the Territorial Band played, the Boy Scouts helped to keep the ring, and the police guarded the fences. As the airman alighted, the sight was awe-inspiring, the crowds seemingly too impressed to speak or cheer. Soon the airman was surrounded by the committee and other prominent spectators, who overwhelmed the dapper, smiling, modest Frenchman with congratulations.

Mr. A. E. Gaved (the hon. secretary), and Messrs. J. Perry, J.P., T. H. Williams, H. Hodge, C.C., Tom J. Smith, H. J. Watkins, J. Pascoe, J. W. Higman, J.P., and H. Varcoe, who, amongst others, as members of the committee and in other ways had made the arrangements, and concerned themselves in the visit of the airman, were prominent in offering a welcome on behalf of the town. M. Salmet was too overwhelmed to say much, and when Mr. J. T. Hawke and some others struck up the French National Anthem, the airman showed his delight by clapping his hands. Juveniles and others crowded around him for autographs and for seats in his aeroplane. Many youngsters were lifted into the machine so as to be able to say they had been in an aeroplane. M. Salmet expressed his delight at the reception, and expressed his cordial thanks for the £10 handed to him by the committee. Mr. Hodge made a felicitous speech, referred to the friendly relations existing between France and England, and to the beneficent influence of the entente cordiale on both countries.

Then the gallant airman gave some exhibition flights, which demonstrated the wonderful power M. Salmet has over his machine and the marvellous evolutions the aeroplane is capable of performing. Afterwards, M. Salmet, again acknowledging the warmth of his reception, gave the order to those holding on to the rear of his machine to let go, and away he sped over the hedge and across the sky, in a few minutes becoming a speck on the horizon towards Fowey, while the huge crowds dispersed, excitedly conversing about the wonderful sight they had witnessed. It was an experience in the lives of those who witnessed it that will never be effaced from the memory, and many thanks are due to those who were mainly instrumental in securing the visit, prominent amongst them being Mr. H. Varcoe, M. Salmet, his manager, and friends passed through the town on Saturday by motor, when they expressed their delight at the suitability of the alighting ground.

An extract from the Cornish Guardian 21st June, 1912

(Rocky Park was used as an airfield by a local aviation company. Returning from the 1914-18 War, Captain Percival Phillips D.F.C. - a native of St. Austell - teamed up with a Mr. Hill to form Hill & Phillips Garage. This firm having serviced the aeroplane engines of a visiting aviation company led to the formation of the Cornwall Aviation Company in 1924 and to the acquisition of an Avro aeroplane. It was only a short distance to tow the fuselages, once their wings had been removed at Rocky Park, to the garage premises in Gover Road, St. Austell.

Rocky Park was also the venue for motor-cycle grass track racing throughout the 1930's, and for a couple of years following the end of the Second World War before the Cornish Stadium was opened at Par Moor in 1949.)

CHAPEL

Religion was held in high esteem in the villages. The chapel was the heart of a village and the centre of its activities, and Sunday Schools were well attended because families were larger in my young days. Their teachers were dedicated men and women, and it seems a great pity that so many Sunday Schools are now closed.

To promote religion, Religious Revival meetings were sometimes called. I remember that the village people were of a very close kind, were helpful to one another and called each other by Christian names. It is so different today - everyone seems to be more individually orientated with only a few trying to promote community spirit.

We used to go (or, rather, _had_ to go !) to Sunday School on Sunday mornings, and to chapel in the evenings. At the end of the service, the preacher would ask for a prayer meeting, which we did not like when we got older as we had other things on our minds ! In the summertime, after chapel, my friends and I would walk to Charlestown, and perhaps over the cliffs to Crinnis to 'chat up' the girls, and then perhaps walk to Biscovey or to St. Blazey Gate.

The two chapels with which I was associated were the Bible Christian Chapel at Tregorrick and the Primitive Methodist Chapel at London Apprentice. I have been told that the Tregorrick chapel, which has been converted into two cottages, was built with stones taken from Menagwins Mine stack. It seems hard to believe now, but I remember when these little chapels were packed with people on Sundays, especially on Sunday School anniversaries. Whit Monday was a big day for the Sunday School children. With a band and large banner, children and parents would march to Trewhiddle House to view the lovely gardens and the big house which, to our eyes, was kept in almost regal state. The children each received a glass of milk and a threepenny bit. They then returned to their tea and sports, with games and a kissing ring. I am sorry that these times will never be seen again.

(Mr. and Mrs. Shilson were depicted in the Cornish Guardian of 20th August, 1909 as "good samaritans to the children of the district". They frequently opened their beautiful gardens to be enjoyed by children. For example, in August 1909, the scholars of All Saints Church, Pentewan, performed a pastoral play for their hosts before having an al fresco tea party, and in August 1913 the girl pupils of Nanpean United Methodist Evening Classes were guests at Trewhiddle, when Mr. and Mrs. Shilson gave 10s. to the class and bags of sweets to the children.)

PRIMITIVE METHODIST CHURCH "BAND OF HOPE AND TEMPERANCE SOCIETY."
NEW MILLS LONDON APPRENTICE. ESTABLISHED 1911.

1915.
OFFICIALS.

PRESIDENT - WILLIAM PRIDEAUX. — GLADYS BICKLEY.
VICE-PRESIDENT - " ANNIE CROCKER. (2)
JOHN DAVIES.
SECRETARY
THOMAS KNOWLES.
TREASURER,
MAY STEPHENS.
CONDUCTOR
SYDNEY CHARLES JURY.
ORGANIST
MAY STEPHENS.

ADULT MEMBERS.

- JENIFER HOSKING.
- ANNIE CROCKER (1)
- MARY ANN STEPHENS.
- E. MAY STEPHENS.
- SARAH PRIDEAUX.
- GERTRUDE STEPHENS.
- GLADYS HODGE.
- DAISY KNOWLES.
- GLADYS BICKLEY.

COMMITTEE.

- WILLIAM PRIDEAUX.
- JOHN DAVIES.
- THOMAS KNOWLES.
- SYDNEY CHARLES JURY.
- JAMES LEAN. 2nd
- JOHN Ed STEPHENS.
- STANLEY WILLIAMS 3rd
- GEORGE MOORE 2nd
- MARY ANN STEPHENS.
- SARAH PRIDEAUX.
- JENIFER HOSKING.
- ANNIE CROCKER (1)
- RUBY BARNICOAT.
- E. MAY STEPHENS.
- ANNIE VIVIAN.
- DAPHNE LIDDICOAT.
- LILLIAN KNOWLES.

- LILLIAN KNOWLES. (1)
- DAPHNE LIDDICOAT.
- RUBY BARNICOAT.
- BESSIE CROSSMAN.
- LILLIAN KNOWLES (2)
- NELLIE LEAN.
- ANNIE VIVIAN.
- FLORA STARKE.
- EMMA KNOWLES.
- ETHEL KNOWLES.
- ELIZABETH CLEMO
- LUISE HODGE.
- ANNIE CROCKER (2)
- SUSIE DAVIES.
- MARY STONE.
- MILLICENT BICKLEY.
- FRANCIS DAVIES.
- OLIVE WILLIAMS.

- WILLIAM PRIDEAUX.
- JAMES LEAK. (2)
- STANLEY WILLIAMS 3rd
- SYDNEY CHARLES JURY.
- THOMAS KNOWLES.
- ALFRED BARNICOAT.
- FRED KEAST.
- ERNEST KNOWLES.
- JOHN E. STEPHENS.
- JOHN DAVIES.
- JOHN HODGE.
- OSWALD BUNGEY.
- LEWIS KNOWLES.
- ANDREW LIDDICOAT.
- GEORGE MOORE. 2nd
- JAMES DAVIES.
- ALGERNON LIDDICOAT.
- STANLEY GOLLEY.

JUNIORS

- GLADYS OLIVER
- WINNIE OLIVER
- OLIVE BENNETT
- ARCHIE BENNETT &
- PEARL OLIVER
- STANLEY OLIVER
- CHARLES OLIVER
- RUBY OLIVER
- FRANK GOLLEY
- LEWIS BECKLEY
- Valenda Thomas Goll.
- JOHN STEPHENS
- ARTHUR STEPHENS
- OLIVE STEPHENS x

JUNIOR MEMBERS.

- OLIVE KNOWLES.
- KATHLEEN CROSSMAN.
- ETHEL LIDDICOAT.
- GLADYS KEAST.
- DOROTHY BICKLEY.
- IVEY LEAN.
- FLORA LEAN.
- LESLIE RABY.
- EDWARD STEPHENS.
- WILLIAM STEPHENS.
- HAROLD LIDDICOAT.
- EDGAR RUNDLE.
- JOHN LEAN.
- FRED LEAN.
- ERNEST KEAST.
- FRANK BICKLEY.
- NORMAN BICKLEY.
- EDWIN BICKLEY.
- CARRIE OLIVER.
- LILLIAN KNOWLES.
- PHYLLIS BICKLEY.
- HARRY OLIVER.
- WILLIAM OLIVER.
- HARRY BICKLEY
- LIZZIE SLEEMAN
- ADA GOLLEY.

Harry Stark

London Apprentice children about to attend New Mills Sunday School Anniversary c. 1931. The buttonholes were customarily provided by Mr. Shilson and, even after his death, were delivered to the village by Mr. Will Crocker, gardener at Trewhiddle, who lived next to the Primitive Methodist Chapel. Left to right are Douglas Oliver, Rodney Stone, Cyril Liddicoat, James Littlejohns, Roy Oliver, Denzil Stone, William Littlejohns.

Harry Stark

Left to right, Back: Jean Beckley, Pearl Oliver, Ruby Oliver. Middle: Queenie Oliver, Hazel Stone. Front: Molly Stone.

59

TREWHIDDLE HOUSE

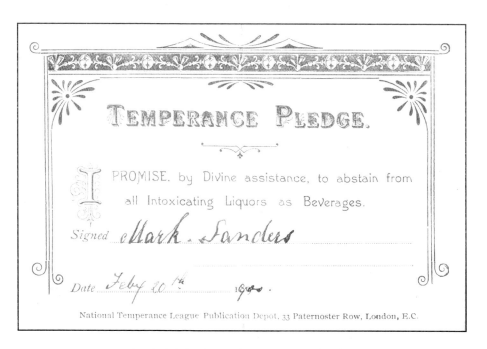

A typical pledge that people were encouraged to sign.

This lovely photograph shows members of New Mills Primitive Methodist Chapel at London Apprentice.
The chapel was built in 1870 and this photograph was taken before the Sunday School was added in 1904.

Mr. Shilson was driven to St. Austell Church by his coachman in a four-wheeled carriage drawn by a pair of horses. He later owned a Rolls Royce. As boys, we had to doff our caps as he passed.

On August Bank Holiday, the Sunday Schools from London Apprentice, Polgooth, Paramoor, Sticker and Trelowth used to go to Pentewan Beach for tea treats, taking tables and forms along with them. They used farm and clay wagons, but the children from St. Austell Sunday Schools used to go by the Pentewan Railway on Thursdays during the summer. They boarded the train at Pondhu, having marched there behind a band - frequently, St. Austell Territorial Band.

(A report in the Cornish Guardian dated 13th July, 1906 stated that the St. Austell Church Sunday School went to Pentewan by railway trucks and returned for tea in Mr. J. Williams' field at Tregorrick. In 1912, the annual treat had to be abandoned because of the weather, and the festivities were later resumed at the Market House, St. Austell, where the children played games and the seniors participated in dancing. Before dismissal, gingerbreads were distributed and there was a scramble for a shower of nuts.)

This Tea Treat was held on 13th July, 1909. The usual venues were Mr. Johnnie Williams' meadow between the junction to Tregorrick and Bluebell Wood below St. Austell, or The Winnick, Pentewan. Both locations gave easy access to the St. Austell & Pentewan Railway, which, through the kindness of Mrs. Johnstone of Trewithen, its owner, provided the necessary transport from the town to the beach at Pentewan.

(Locomotive and General Railway Photographs)
National Railway Museum, York.

"Canopus" pulling wagons loaded with passengers bound for Pentewan Beach. Photographed at Pentewan reservoirs on 8th July, 1915, the wind pump and tank for supplying water to the engines are clearly visible.

A St. Austell Outing.

TRIP TO PENTEWAN DESCRIBED.

The scene was Pon-dhu, and the time last Thursday afternoon. By the old bridge, which spans the St. Austell River at the lower end of the town, a score or so of quaint little wooden waggons, that spoke in unmistakeable terms of their connection with the china clay trade, were drawn up in a long line on the miniature mineral railway that runs down the Pentewan Valley; and the tiny engine, to which the waggons were attached, sent out great volumes of nauseating smoke, and puffed and snorted alternately. All along the line the scene was one of bustle and excitement, and the very air rang with the happy laughter of children, and the pleasant banter of mature matrons, whose spirits overflowed with the jollity of the occasion of the expectation of joys to come.

It was the occasion of the annual outing of the St. Austell Baptist Sunday School to Pentewan, and the long-looked-for hour of departure was at hand.

Not the slightest intention had I of joining the 1,000 odd men and women and children who made up this gigantic picnic party, but—well! the sight of this happy throng on pleasure bent was too much for one who is ever ready to part company with work, and no sooner had the cry "take your seats" been uttered than I—without thinking for a moment of the things that had been decided for me to do that afternoon—found myself in the midst of a pushing, jostling, screaming crowd, all scrambling for a place in the waggons.

"Take your seats" someone had shouted, and it was the best joke of the day. The particular waggon in which I had been cast like a fish in a net with so many dozen others boasted a couple of forms, but "first come, first served," is always the rule on such occasions, and Mrs. Brown and Mrs. Brown's sister and another lady equally as great as the others as far as proportion goes occupied one, and the other was warped almost to breaking point under the weight of four old dames, whose names I would not mention for worlds. The rest of us—and we could be counted by dozens—had the centre of the waggon "all to ourselves," and while the band played "The Sea is England's Glory" or something like it, we were huddled together like the proverbial sardines in a box. The commotion up and down the line was considerable.

Those who had found standing places after the general rush shouted "No room" until they were well-nigh hoarse, but late comers were not to be denied, and clamoured around the doors of the waggons until by means of much wriggling and squeezing they climbed inside, in the midst of occupants whose reception was none too hearty.

We had taken in so many since our waggon was declared to be overcrowded that Mrs. Brown worked herself into a state of white heat, which is a surprising thing to say, considering how old she was, but her views on the subject of overcrowding and people generally were expressed with such warmth that no other term adequately describes the condition of her temper. Mrs. Brown's sister, a very respectable widow, according to her own confession, was somewhat older, and, of course, bigger than Mrs. Brown, but she was not in the least disturbed. She seemed to revel in the crush, but she knew what she was about, for when we started she gave place to a gentleman friend, and found what appeared to be a comfortable seat on his knee.

It seemed to most of us an eternity before we started. Many a time we occupants of No. 14 waggon shouted "All ready" to the driver and nodded our heads, winked knowingly, and motioned him onwards by waving our hands frantically in the air. But that important individual took no notice whatever. Mrs. Brown would not be ignored, so in her most shrill and penetrating voice she demanded to know the cause of the delay, and then the whole thing was explained by a passenger in the next waggon, who spoke, through a megaphone made up of an old newspaper, what some said was the truth and others not. Bill Jones, he said, had come down arrayed in cream flannels—that had come to him as a present — and his chapel-going coat, but unfortunately at the very last moment Bill discovered that he had left his pipe behind. As everyone was aware of the fact that Bill and his pipe were inseparable, word was passed forward to wait until Bill's return, which would be within a minute. When a good many minutes had gone, and Bill had not re-appeared, someone volunteered to go in search of him, and away he went also. He was barely lost to view when another imagined he possessed the influence necessary to induce Bill to return quicker than the other, and with that object in view started off. Bill returned a second or so afterwards, and from the first waggon to the last it was known that he had recovered his pipe, and that it was doing its work faithfully and well. In the meantime, while a boy was despatched to bring the two absentees back, the discovery was made that a diminutive creature was in danger of being left behind, and from the centre of the grassy plot at the rear, where it was having a picnic on its own, a baby girl was lifted into the brawny arms of a tripper, and borne down the line of the waggons in search of its mother. How many girls from 13 to 16, and toothless old dames ranging from 60 to 75 shook their heads when the question was put to them, "Is this yours?" I would not dare to say, for I lost count, but I know that the 19th waggon had been reached before a claimant for the child could be found, and just at that moment the two wanderers came rushing back in a state of utter exhaustion leading the boy! between them.

Then we started off, and how funny it all was. The shrill whistle of the engine was as nothing compared with the cry that went up from the thousand odd throats as the train began to move, and the laughter that followed completely drowned the shrieking of the unoiled wheels and the grinding and creaking of the rusty old brakes.

Bump, bump, bump went the waggons, and those of us who stood fell into each other's arms, which was very nice in some cases, and very bad in others, and toppled over and crushed those who occupied the seats. Mrs. Brown was on the verge of fainting, but her sister took advantage of the opportunity to cling closer to him on whose knee she sat, which after all was the proper thing to do. The girl in the pink sun-bonnet giggled again, as if she were well pleased with the proceedings, but her smiles were turned into frowns when she realised that her jewellery had suffered in the crush, and that the bangle on her bare arm was neither round nor square. In other waggons there was similar commotion. Old women struggled to regain their equilibrium in a heated scramble for their bonnets; holiday making veterans of toil bobbed their hairless heads into the faces of young girls; dimpled cheeks rubbed against bearded chins, and smarted as the result; and the child in the corner, munching an apple, was nearly choked. Such was the scene in the waggons when we started, and all the way down the lovely valley we swayed to and fro, and fell against each other and laughed and cried for joy as we went rattling merrily along.

Pentewan was bathed in golden glory when we arrived. The heather-clad cliffs, the green and yellow sward, the fine stretch of sand, and the sea, like a mirrored lake beyond, all made a charming and delightful scene.

When everybody had alighted, and the various articles necessary to a picnic, such as umbrellas, paper bags, baskets, and bottles with coloured liquid in them, had been collected, and restored as near as possible to their rightful owners, we rushed pell-mell to the beach, and each did his or her best to look unconcerned in trying to out do the others in a race for the water's edge. Until the welcome calls to tea were heard the majority disported themselves like children out from school, but some there were whose only thoughts were of the tea, and lest they should be forestalled and turned empty away they clung to the seats that flanked the uncovered tables, and waited patiently while the cloths were laid, the provisions set out, and the water boiled. In batches we sat down to tables erected in a grassy enclosure, where the sun, pouring down with torrid heat, melted the butter and dried up the "splits" and saffron cake. Whether it was by accident or design it is difficult to say, but Mrs. Brown and her friends were included in our party, and while we cleared the dishes, time and again, of good things that were set out in a straight line down the centre of the table, her pleasant chatter produced such mirth that not a few narrowly escaped choking, and many ladies spilled the tea over their cream blouses, which made them feel uncomfortable for the remainder of the day.

Tea was quickly over, much too soon for a good many, but such epithets as "Hurry up there," "Have'e bought the lot," and "What appetites they've got," flung at you by a hungry crowd outside the enclosure is not conducive to a bumper tea, so a few of us surreptiously stowed away in our pockets what there wasn't time to eat, and vacated the table for the benefit of others.

To write of the enjoyments participated in by the crowd would require more space than is available, but there were no visible mishaps, and when the hour for the return journey arrived lovers came out of their trysting places, bathers got into civilised attire, and husbands, who had managed to evade the watchful eyes of their better halves, appeared once more on the scene, and we met again, a happy family, at the mineral railway terminus.

It is surprising how you increase in numbers when you go to Pentewan. We had come down about a thousand of us, but the crowd that waited to be given a ride back, free gratis, and for nothing, was very little short of 1,500.

"Explain to me the cause of the increase," I said to a man, and he replied "Easy enough. Some people walk down from St. Austell; others come by 'busses and other ways, bring their teas, and have a ride home again. We take 'em along, but it's a terrible crush."

So it proved, and the squeezing we had at Pond-dhu was not to be compared with that with which we began the return journey, and when the twenty waggons packed tighter than they had even been before there was left in the road a congregation that no preacher would despise. But none were left behind. More waggons were put on for the little engine to draw, and just as darkness set in steam was got up, and homewards we started. Away down at the rear a sweet singer started "Lead kindly light," and the grand old hymn swelled in volume as it swept up the waggons until Mrs. Brown chimed in with her shrill soprano and her sister's friend his under-ground bass, and then the sound was deafening.

In the hush that followed the sound of voices was heard in the distance, and we assured each other that the journey was almost at an end. A few minutes and then the train came to a standstill. Our trip was over, and tired out but supremely happy we turned our faces homewards.

A. S.

An extract from the Cornish Guardian
25th August, 1911

Harry Stark

Members of New Mills Primitive Methodist Chapel at a Tea Treat at the southern end of Pentewan Beach in the 1930's. Members of the Liddicoat, Oliver and Stephens families, in particular, can be identified enjoying their traditional saffron buns, which were usually the size of small plates ! In my boyhood years, the Tea Treats following the Whit Sunday Chapel Anniversary at London Apprentice were held on Whit Monday either in the meadow opposite the Chapel ("Jane's Field"), or in the field opposite the former London Apprentice Inn ("Mrs. Kelly's").

NEW MILLS PRIMITIVE METHODIST CHAPEL

Reproduced from the 1881 Edition of the Ordnance Survey

LONG-SINCE DISAPPEARED

In the town of St. Austell, many old buildings have been demolished.

There were two terraces of old houses just off the top of East Hill which were known as "The Rag" or "Carvath" - a place where I, as a boy, used to think the roughs and bullies lived ! *(Two terraces which ran parallel with the present-day Albert Road - then known as Back Lane - were actually called Greenwoods Row and they existed on the site now occupied by a children's amusement centre.)*

Further down East Hill, two other parallel terraces of houses, both known as Merrifields Row, existed on the site of the present telephone exchange. *(The present butcher's shop is the only remaining part of the northernmost terrace.)*

Below Merrifields Row was Paul's Square, with cottages on its east, west and southern sides. These buildings were demolished to make way for a motor-car sales and service business.

J. W. & S. St. Austell

The outer terrace of Merrifield's Row is on the right-hand side of the picture, with the north-east corner of Paul's Square just visible.

Duke Street used to be a much narrower road than it is today, with small, dark cottages on its higher side situated in what is now the centre of the present thoroughfare. *(During demolition at the site of these cottages in the summer of 1913, a serious accident occurred when a workman by the name of Reed was buried by a falling wall.)*

This building on the corner of South Street (Hotel Road) and Church Street was used, amongst other things, as St. Austell Bank, the Corn Exchange, and a branch of the County Library. Two photographs taken by Mr. Roy Dutch have been used as the basis of this view. I have interpreted the remaining facade from small detail on picture-postcards and from aerial photography.

The Corn Exchange adjacent to the White Hart Hotel was demolished in 1960 to enable the upper part of South Street to be widened.

In North Street, which used to be known as Menacuddle Street, many small cottages have been pulled down. In Priory Row, also, several houses and two long terraces of houses have made way for what, today, is the Priory Car Park.

I remember when there were houses and cottages in South Street all the way down to where Trinity Street is now. Beyond Trinity Street, the lower part of what is now South Street was called Kiln Lane, and I can still visualise the terrace of seven houses on the western side above Moorland Road. *(Before the St. Austell Bypass was built, Kiln Lane forked into two roads, one leading into Trewhiddle and the other extending southwards down to the St. Austell Moors and the Pentewan Valley. My father's great-grandfather once worked the old lime kiln situated adjacent to the St. Austell & Pentewan Railway line on the site of the present B & Q carpark fronting Pentewan Road. This is why, presumably, the lower section of what is South Street today was once known as Kiln Lane.)*

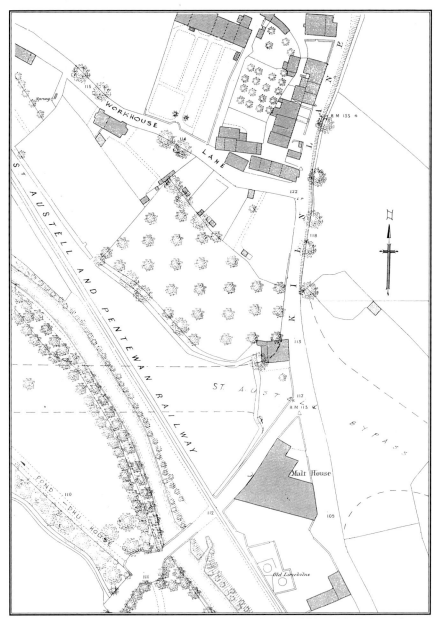

Reproduced from the 1881 Edition of the Ordnance Survey

The position of the A.390 St. Austell Bypass has been superimposed on this plan, which shows Kiln Lane and Workhouse Lane (now Moorland Road, so-called because it led towards St. Austell Moors in the Pentewan Valley). Note the position of the lime kilns which, even in 1881, were described as "old". They were erected in approximately 1830.

Moorland Road, formerly called Workhouse Lane, has altered a lot. I well remember Charlie Freeman's Rag and Bone Store occupying a fairly large site. As children, we used to take our rabbit skins there, and we were given a halfpenny or a penny for each of them. There was a house run by John Ivey as a common lodging house, and further along there was a heap of granite stones which were the ruins of the old foundry. Houses at each end of Moorland Road have been pulled down, and a square the boys used to call Whitechapel has made way for the flats at the bottom of West Hill. The Health Clinic now stands where Birchalls, the show people, lived.

I know of three public houses which no longer exist. Two of them were in Hotel Road - The Graham Arms, and The Tap at the rear of the White Hart. The third was the Dog's Hole in Menacuddle Street.

(In November 1907, the attention of the Market Commissioners was drawn to the state of the pig market at the rear of the Graham Arms, particularly during the warm summer months. It was situated in the midst of dwelling houses, and the lack of proper sanitary arrangements caused a nuisance to the local inhabitants.

The Graham Arms opened its doors for the last time on Friday, 14th August 1914, its licence having been cancelled.)

The little alley *(still in existence)* which went from Hotel Road to Church Street was known as Buggy Alley.

The town was well served by blacksmith's shops, namely, Harry Jenkins on part of the site now occupied by Woolworths; Ebenezer Scott's behind the present Post Office in High Cross Street; Daniels in Beech Road; George Jewell in Trenance Road, and 'Tut' (Thomas) Smith's in Blowinghouse Hill.

At the top of West Hill, between Charles Bennett's cloam china shop and Billy Thomas' grocers shop was an archway entrance to Burton Court. These buildings were demolished in the early sixties to enable Trinity Street to be constructed.

The United Methodists chapel in East Hill is now the British Legion Club. *(Since this was written, the British Legion has, of course, moved to premises in Duke Street and the building itself was pulled down when the new road was constructed between East Hill and South Street.)* The Primitive Methodist chapel building in South Street was demolished when that part of the town was redeveloped and the street widened. Some people may remember this chapel in South Street as the Faraday Hall, it being used in its later years as a South Western Electricity Board warehouse.

Great Western Railway delivery vans and wagons were at one time kept at the bottom of South Street.

Where St. Austell Cattle Market is situated, there was once a cowshed and fields, from which Ernie Biddick daily drove his cows to Tregorrick to graze.

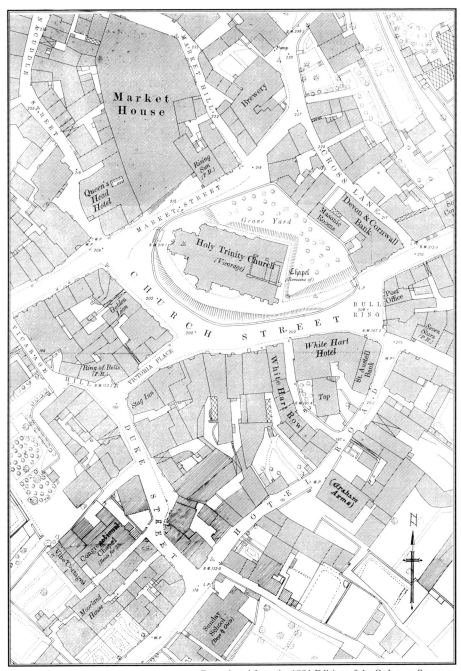

Reproduced from the 1881 Edition of the Ordnance Survey

71

Aerofilms

Posted from St. Austell in 1929, this postcard shows on the left-hand side St. Austell Central School, the Baptist Church and Burton Place off West Hill. Above Burton Place, on the edge of the photograph, some of the houses in Priory Row are visible. Centre top is the former brick building at St. Austell Railway Station. The Odeon Cinema had not been built, but the nearby New Inn (at the rear of what is now Woolworths) can be seen.

Further down the valley, between the cattle market and Watering Lane, was St. Austell's old cricket field. There were four cottages opposite the cricket field and in one of these lived Mac Grose, to whom I have referred earlier.

I can remember St. Austell Council refuse dump at Menagwins as a small heap, and saw it grow over the years to a huge mound. I then saw the whole area graded and flattened over a swamp to make way for a new sewerage works. All the rubbish and rubble was carried in carts and wagons, as was coal.

A tragedy occurred within our family in July 1907. My sister, Winnifred, and my brother, Edward, were poisoned after eating contaminated walnut chocolates which they had found whilst playing on the refuse tip. My sister, who was six years old, died of 'ptomaine poisoning' but, fortunately, my brother recovered.

There used to be water taps in some streets, where cottagers obtained their household water. There were no indoor toilets in those days, so at night a chamberpot was commonly used, and secreted under the bed. There was no gas or electric lighting, and oil lamps were used when reading and writing as well as for general illumination. We used to take a candle in a candlestick holder to light our way when we went to bed.

COMMERCE & THE WAY OF LIFE

The production of china clay is the main industry around St. Austell. I do, of course, remember the Clay Strike of 1913 and some of the men who took part in it, and also seeing the Glamorgan Police who were sent here to quell it.

I remember the old clay wagons and cask wagons, with their two and three horse teams; the wagoners with their cracking whips and words of command - "Whoick mear" to go to the left, and "Gee Back" to go to the right, which the horses knew and slowly did. Iron drags were put on the wheels to act as brakes when the wagons were going downhill with full loads.

The wagoners could get their pints of beer at the General Wolfe public house through one of the windows opening onto Bodmin Road. These wagoners were tough, hard-working men and handled tons of clay a day with large, long-handled shovels. Some of these men would have had smallholdings or farms to look after as well, so you might say that they were fourteen-days-a-week men !

The Photocrom Co. Ltd.

A typical scene in Fore Street, where, prior to St. Austell Bypass being built in the 1920's, scores of such heavily-laden wagons passed through daily en route for Charlestown from the hinterland of St. Austell.

The clay wagons used to come from the clayworks through St. Austell Fore Street to the White Hart Hotel, where they had to stop in preparation for the pull up East Hill. The wagoners worked with a pair of wagons, with two horses to a wagon, until they came to East Hill and then they doubled up to four horses up front to haul one wagon up the hill. Then the horses were brought back to bring up the second wagon. The wagoners were strong men, and generally appeared to know how to treat the horses well. There were many tales about an old wagoner and one story was that one day after carrying coal all day, he went home to 'The Rag' at the top of East Hill, his face being as black as soot. Later that evening, he went to the butchers for some meat. The butcher said, "Hello, just left work ?" "Oh no," said the wagoner, "I bin 'ome a long while." The butcher said, "Well, I thought you would have washed and tidied up by now," to which the wagoner replied, "Aw, no, I'm on cawl 'gain morrah !" Another story was that one day he was wanted on the telephone and was called over to answer it. The caller kept saying, "Are you there ? Are you there ?" The wagoner replied, "Course I'm 'ere, I'm noddin' ent I ?"

St. Austell Church.

The Bull Ring, pictured here in 1920, often became congested with the number of wagons waiting for extra horses to become available to help pull the heavy loads up East Hill.

Police and Clay Waggoners.

—:o:—

[TO THE EDITOR.]

Sir,—The question regarding the very strin-gent conditions under which clay waggoners who, in their daily routine, have to pass through the streets of St. Austell, are at present labouring is one which should appeal to every reader of this paper. As every-one knows china clay is the staple industry of Mid-Cornwall, and without it St. Austell and the surrounding villages would become almost nonentities. Yet, in spite of this, the poor driver of a clay waggon is driven from pillar to post. and looked on in the town almost as an undesirable. A new trial has now been added to the lot of these un-fortunate individuals in the form of an official order that all coupling up shall be done in the Bull Ring instead of at East Hill. Probably ever since clay has been conveyed through St. Austell streets the clay waggons have been drawn up at the bottom of East Hill, until a fellow waggoner has come along. and then by the united efforts of the horses from both waggons the wag-gon is got up the hill. No one will deny that this coupling up business in a town like St. Austell is a nuisance, yet it has to be done, for no two or three ordinary horses can draw the waggons, loaded as they are. up such steep ascents without help. Then if it has to be done why not do it where the least inconvenience is caused? Under the present conditions the Bull Ring is blocked morning and afternoon, and it is no rare occurrence to see eight to ten waggons drawn up in this, the main thor-oughfare in the town. It is obvious that the police—for the new arrangements are by their orders—would be much better advised to let the waggoners continue to halt at the bottom of the hill as heretofore.

Apart from the fact that the waggoners who have no easy task to negotiate their cumbersome vehicles through the narrow streets, are placed at a decided disadvan-tage by the new order, when one takes into consideration that three streets adjoin the Bull Ring, besides the main entrance to the town from the station, it must be admit-ted that the ruling of the authorities in this case is decidedly erratic.

CLAYBOY.

St. Austell, July, 1908.

An extract from the Cornish Guardian 10th July, 1908

When I was a boy, people had larger families than today and so the older girls of the family had to go out to work - often "in service" as it was called - to help provide the money to raise their younger brothers and sisters at home. This usually meant that they left their homes and lived at the place of work. Here, they were under a kind of serfdom, having to do work of all kinds in the household from morning until night. Some had to dress to order, in the morning having to wear clothes suitable for their work, and, in the afternoon, having to change and put on a black dress and a white cap. Their hours were long and their time off was short; they usually had one afternoon a week off (generally, Wednesdays), from about 2.00 p.m. until about 9.30 or 10.00 p.m. when they had to return to work. The First World War altered this a lot, with women being asked to volunteer for war service; and, again, in World War Two, an even bigger call was made on women.

In my boyhood days, some old people lived on the Parish Pay, and if they could not manage on this, they were sent to the Union (Workhouse) to end their days. Thankfully, those days have now gone. I remember the hostility that was shown when the Old Age Pensions Bill was being brought in, which made an allowance of five shillings a week. One gentleman said it would "weaken the moral fibre of the nation !"

(The Old Age Pensions Act of 1908 would have applied to approximately 4,000 persons in Cornwall, a figure which represented $1^{1}/4\%$ of the county's population who had reached the qualifying age of 70 years.

In January 1909, the Cornish Guardian carried an article on "the 500 'veterans of industry' who had, during the past week, received at the hands of the State the pensions so long promised. Realisation had dispelled all doubts in the minds of those poor old souls who, up to the last, declared that it was too good to be true. 1st January, 1909 will remain for all time as a landmark in the history of Liberal governments and as an epoch-making period in British politics worthy to be ranked with the Repeal of the Corn Laws and the Great Reform Act".

Some people, however, were still very much against the giving of Old Age Pensions. They felt it was unfair that those people who had made provisions by saving for their old age would not receive pensions, whilst those who had been "thriftless and intemperate" would also receive the allowance.)

SUFFRAGETTES AT ST. AUSTELL.

—:o:—

HECKLED ABOUT THEIR TACTICS.

—:o:—

THEIR OPPOSITION TO THE GOVERNMENT RESENTED.

—:o:—

"Votes for Women," afterwards changed by a joker to "Work for Women," in chalk letters on the pavements stared St. Austell people in the face again on Monday morning announcing to all and sundry that the suffragists had once more arrived to give voice to their sentiments.

Punctually at the announced time Miss James (Bristol) stood upon the steps leading to the church and faced a little knot of interested spectators. As "chairman" of the meeting, and, in introducing Miss Mary Phillips, she remarked that they had been called "hooligans" and "the wild women of Westminster." Their actions against the Government were ones which would be taken against any Government that refused the vote to women. They would use the same policy against the next Government if they did not give them the vote, and they would get a worse time than the Liberal Government had at present. They only asked for the vote on the same terms as the men had it.

Miss Phillips, a former resident of St. Austell, prefaced a long address with a resume of their policy. They were not asking for a privilege, but what was their right. They demanded the vote because they paid their taxes, and because a great many laws were unjust to women. They did not propose that the women should have the power to make the laws, for that would be unjust to the men. (Laughter.) They did not want to take anything away from the men, but the best men in the world could not understand the point of view of women. The point of view of both men and women was wanted to get an ideal state of things, and they demanded the vote so that the interest of women might be safeguarded. Women were doing a noble self-sacrificing work in temperance reform and social work, but the vote was the only effective weapon by which they could bring about these reforms. Some 400 women had suffered imprisonment. (A Voice: "That is your own fault.") We should not do it unless we thought it worth while.

"PESTERING THE GOVERNMENT."

On referring to the opposition of the Government to votes for women, the speaker was interrupted with the remark: "What about the House of Lords?" "We do not know what the Lords will do," was the reply. (A Voice: Don't they find the money for you?") "That is an old story; our money comes from all political parties in the country." (A Voice: "Chiefly the Tories.") "We don't ask you what your politics are when we take up a collection." (A Voice: "Do you ever oppose the Tories?") "No, because they are not in power. We oppose the Government in power." (A Voice: "You are opposing your friends.") "But the Liberals are the people to go to. We are determined to pester them as much as we can." (Mr. Vincent: More pestering than opposing; that is one of your greatest mistakes — your pestering. You used the right word.") "We oppose them by whatever means we can." ("No, you pester them, stick to the right word.") "The late Sir H. Campbell-Bannerman said 'Keep on agitating and pestering.'" (Cries of "No, no," and "We will not have that.") "I can give you chapter and verse. If you do not wish to hear what I have to say—("Why do you pester Cabinet Ministers and not allow them to speak?") "Because they will not give us the vote." ("And you expect better treatment because you are women?") "Why did you not ask the Tories?" was another question?" "Because the Liberals are the people who professed to believe in freedom and democracy. Let them carry our Bill, and if the House of Lords reject it they (the Liberals) will have our help to fight the House of Lords. We shall oppose the next Government if we don't get the vote." ("No you won't.") Continuing, Miss Phillips said no matter how long they were imprisoned it would make no difference to their agitation, for they did not lack the spirit and courage of British men.

POINTED QUESTIONS ABOUT SUFFRAGETTE TACTICS.

Questions being invited, it was asked —Why do you oppose the Liberal candidate and support the Tory candidate?

We never support any candidate in any election. ("Oh!")

Did you not oppose the Liberal candidate in Devon?

We simply oppose the Government. (Boos and "Oh!")

You are working for the Tories?

We are working for no party whatever.

Mr. Vincent: Don't you understand that you are opposing the party likely to give you the vote, and supporting the party who are not going to give you the vote? I am a supporter of votes for women under certain conditions.

We do not support any party. Oh! no, you may not believe it.

No; we shall not allow you to speak unless you are candid.

I am absolutely candid. I could not speak without I am absolutely convinced. Actions speak louder than words, and we refuse to believe in the Government's sympathy unless they do something to show it.

If they made you a false promise you would believe it.

Do you think you Liberal party would make a false promise? We demand a definite promise. ("You have had it from Mr. Lloyd George, and yet you oppose him.")

Mr. T. Barnicoat: My friends say I am afraid to ask you a question.

Miss Phillips: I am sure you are not. (Laughter.) (Voices: "You are telling lies, Mr. Barnicoat.")

Mr. Barnicoat: Why do you restrict the franchise to women property owners?

We do not restrict the franchise. Our present franchise qualifications have been laid down by the men and not the women. (Laughter.) If they are good enough for men they are for women.

Mr. Barnicoat: I am not opposed to you or your society, but some of your tactics are disgusting. Are you in favour of the vote for women lodgers?

Of course, I am, and demand the vote on the same terms as the men.

At the close of the meeting Mr. Vincent said, although he was a supporter of the movement, he felt they were making a great mistake. The franchise was never obtained except on constitutional lines.

In the evening the suffragettes again addressed a large crowd at the same place. During the meeting two bags of pepper were thrown, but caused no inconvenience, except a few sneezes. There were several questions.

An extract from the Cornish Guardian
20th August, 1909

General Elections caused a great deal of excitement in St. Austell. In January 1910, Lloyd George visited the town, and a fortnight later Winston Churchill gave a speech in the Market House. *(The Liberal M.P. for the St. Austell Division of Cornwall during my father's boyhood was a Mr. W.A. McArthur. He represented this part of the county from 1887 until 1908, after having defeated the highly-popular Cornishman, Mr. E.W. Brydges-Wylliams.)*

S. Dalby-Smith, St. Blazey

THE CORNISH MP's.

CROYDON MARKS ESQ MP.

HON T AGAR ROBARTES MP.

G. HAY-MORGAN ESQ MP.

WE ARE SEVEN

W. A. McARTHUR ESQ MP.

ONE AND ALL

J. BARKER ESQ MP.

A.E. DUNN ESQ MP.

CLIFFORD J CORY ESQ MP.

There was no Milk Marketing Board or Unigate Dairies in my day and we used to get our milk from small dairies and milk carts which went around the town. Amongst others, there were Jones of Nanphysick Farm, Roberts of Mulvra, Williams of Tregorrick and Jelbert of Trewhiddle. Some dairies which I remember were Lawry of Hotel Road, Truscott of West Bridge, Grigg of Truro Road, Stephens of Priory and Clift of East Hill. Milk delivery to the Union Workhouse and 'Scattered Homes' was let out to tender to milkmen or farmers. They delivered milk to a girls home at Lower Trewhiddle, a boys home in South Street by the present roundabout on the bypass, and homes in Tregonissey Road and Slades Road.

Gone are the days of delivery carts and wagons, traps of corn merchants, butchers, bakers, greengrocers, fish jowters and ironmongers, and cherry, plum and apple carts. Mail was collected by mail-traps and mail-carts and often delivered locally the same day.

Gone are the days, too, when butchers drove cattle to the slaughterhouses straight from the farms. Cattle from Gorran or Caerhayes were sometimes driven to Pengrugla by the farmers and then were taken by the butchers to the slaughterhouses.

J. Toullec, Mevagissey

This interesting postcard, sent from Mevagissey in 1915, shows a horse-operated hay-pole in use, hoisting hay up to the top of the huge rick. The pony-trap bears the owner's name of Kendall, Bodrugan, Gorran.

During the course of my work, I used to deliver meat in a horse-drawn covered wagon, and one of my rounds took me as far west as Sticker and Hewaswater.

The butchery business, combined with the farm at Tregorrick, meant I had to work long and irregular hours, especially when animals had to be fetched for slaughter, and the hay harvest had to be "saved".

(Anyone who has ever had responsibility for gathering in a good hay crop will understand the appropriateness of the use of this word. Usually four consecutive drying days are required for the moisture in grass to dry sufficiently, and dry weather conditions for this length of time are not always available. If the weather 'broke', a crop of hay could be lying in the field and deteriorating for a week or more, and this would greatly increase the amount of labour involved in the drying. The process of gathering the dried crop into huge ricks that were built in those days was very time-consuming and labour-intensive and naturally required good weather conditions.

My father, in addition to his full-time job, kept a couple of cows, a fat bullock, pigs and poultry, and saved his own hay in his 'spare' time. He would mow a meadow of hay, or some of it, before and after work, and he considered this to be part of his normal way of life.)

The R.A.P. Co. Ltd.

Fore Street, Sticker, c. 1937. The two ladies talking outside the Post Office are Mrs. Dorothy Matthews and Miss Eileen Broad.

A view of Hewaswater c. 1905, looking westward from the junction with the road to Lower Sticker. The two little girls pictured were Violet and Rosalind Lean.

Miss Jemimah Kendall standing in the doorway of her shop at Hewaswater, which was situated on the corner of the site of the present Hewaswater General Engineering Ltd. The shop was later used by Mr. Jack Best for men's hairdressing.

Mevagissey inner harbour at the turn of the century, as depicted in this postcard posted in 1907.

Fish from Mevagissey was brought to St. Austell Station by a wagon and two horses. In the summer evenings, young men from Mevagissey would travel on the wagons for a joy-ride, and the Pentewan valley would ring with the sounds of their singing voices.

I think of the doctors going in carriages to see their patients, the trades of coopers, bootmakers, blacksmiths, wheel-wrights and saddlers, most of which have now gone; also the old ostlers who looked after the horses and the barrow-men who wheeled their barrows with the goods of commercial travellers.

I can remember travelling craftsmen, such as knife grinders, scissors sharpeners, mat menders, umbrella menders and tinsmiths. St. Austell had its own travelling tinsmith, old Eli Brown. His son, also Eli Brown, was a blacksmith by trade and won many prizes at the Royal Cornwall Shows for the shoeing of horses.

In the summertime, the streets of St. Austell had a water cart to dampen the dust, there being no tarmacadam surfacing in my younger days. I well recall the old lamplighter in St. Austell going around with his long stick to light the street lamps, which were then fuelled by gas.

Cloke's Bus on Town Bridge, Mevagissey. In the summer of 1908, the Great Western Railway Road Motor Service was inaugurated, and Pentewan saw the first appearance of the Great Western Motor "Car" in August. This service greatly affected the trade of the horse-drawn buses. An amusing incident was recorded in 1911, when a newsboy jumped onto a bus laden with passengers at St. Austell Station. The boy rang the bell in the absence of a conductor, and the driver only realised he had no conductor when he reached Porthpean !

People from Mevagissey could travel to and from St. Austell by various buses. Horse-drawn buses were owned by Cloke, Elvins, and Cragg, the latter's slogan being "Always Room for One more !" - but one had to walk up the hills ! Motor-buses were later introduced - Cloke's "La Première" and Bishop & Elvins' "Duchess of Cornwall".

The Coastguards were relocated from time to time, and I remember often seeing men and their families with their possessions en route to a new posting.

I can recollect the Royal Naval Volunteer Reservists being called up on one fine Sunday for service in the First World War. *(The Cornish Guardian of 31st July, 1914 confirmed the fears of war breaking out, and the following week there were reports of the reservists having been called up and leaving St. Austell, and of the Coastguards being the next to be called to arms.)*

St. Austell had its own corn mills, one of which was Treleaven's Mill at the bottom of East Hill. The access to this mill was through an archway between the old Post Office *(now Roy Dutch's photographic shop)* and Worthington's Shop. There was a mill in Moorland Road, which was worked by a large water wheel, and also a mill at Pondhu.

These two postcards show Pondhu Mill and the miller's cottage as they were in 1912. These premises, last worked as a corn mill by Farm Industries in 1970, were at one time Lower Blowinghouse (smelting) and a candle factory.

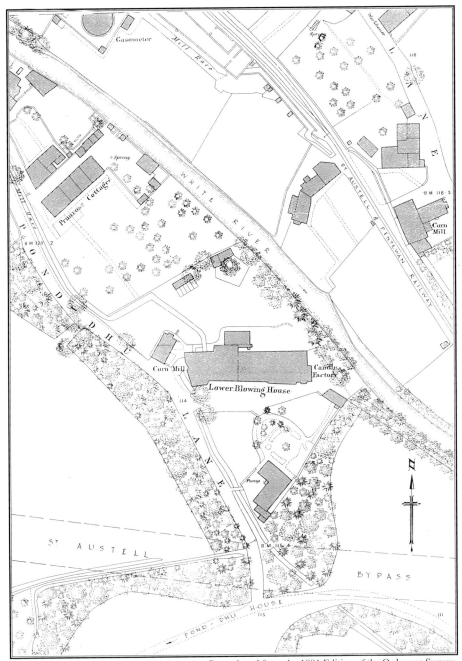

Reproduced from the 1881 Edition of the Ordnance Survey

87

H. Gibbs, St. Austell

A Mr. or Mrs. Davis of West Bridge posted this card in November 1909 and said that "Clarence is on the bridge, but you can't see much of him". The sluices in the centre of the scene controlled the water which powered Pondhu Mill.

In the Pentewan valley, opposite the junction to Watering Lane, there was a mica-dry. Water was taken from the river through a sluice by West Bridge and conveyed via a leat to two settling pits behind the old lime kiln. Just beside the dry, the brothers Philip and Jack Giles forded the river with their clay wagons to reach their stables. Philip Giles' house was known as "Moorlake Cottage," Pentewan Road.

My father was put into "farm service", as it was called, at the age of nine, and being poor in those days, he did not have a change of clothing should his normal wear become saturated during heavy rain. He was unable to read or write.

Two great-uncles of mine told me that when they were boys they helped to unload the limestone barges at the kiln on the southern end of Pentewan beach near Sconhoe Farm. The kiln is some distance from the sea today, and when one looks at the accumulation of sand on the beach, one can see the vast quantity of effluent from the china clay workings that has been brought down by the River Vinnick (White River).

I also had an uncle who, as a young man, used to walk from Bodelva, near St. Blazey Gate, to Dowgas Tin Mine, near Coombe, and walk home again after carrying out a day's work there !

Another uncle of mine went to sea as a small boy, and he said that when he started his career he was only just tall enough to put the kettle on the galley stove. He went to Newfoundland in the old wooden schooners to bring home cod fish. He later became a boatswain on the P. & O. liners. The hard times that many of my relatives endured did not seem to injure their health seriously. Most of them lived to be old men and they seemed contented with life.

Some of the old folks I knew were real characters and, as such, attracted nicknames by which they were generally known. Three uncles of mine were known as Jinny, Bimse, and Rat. There were the three Parsons brothers and they were known as Prickly, Muskey and Toddy. There were "Strikefire" Bennett, "Bonar" Stone, "Bulldog" Rowe and many others, all of whom were very good workmen. Amongst the many stonemasons responsible for the lovely stone hedging still to be seen in Sawles Road and elsewhere in St. Austell were Charlie Kinnear, Messrs. Sanders, Clemo, Clemes, Allen, Abbott, Blamey, Oliver, Chesterfield, Jacobs and Caff, and the Kent brothers.

My father told me that the captains of the sailing ships at Charlestown used to walk along the cliffpaths to assess weather conditions, there being no weather forecasts available in those days !

Designed by John Smeaton, the engineer, Charlestown was built between 1791 and 1801 and financed by Charles Rashleigh primarily for the export of china clay. As copper mining increased, this ore was also exported, and coal, timber and ironwork for the mines were imported. The village which grew up around the port sustained all the trades associated with shipping and fishing. A leat was constructed to convey water for flushing the dock from Luxulyan, approximately seven miles distant. This photograph was taken prior to 1909, when the 1st January edition of the Cornish Guardian carried an article on the opening of the mammoth clay dry at Charlestown.

At the time when St. Austell Foundry was working at West Hill, there was an apprentice whom I knew called Davey. He lived at Moorland Road and he later carried out a great deal of the engineering work for the Commerce Mine near Sticker.

PENTEWAN VALLEY & THE ST. AUSTELL AND PENTEWAN RAILWAY

The River Vinnick flowing through the valley rises in the "higher quarters" of St. Austell *(near Hensbarrow)* and reaches the sea at Pentewan. It used to be bordered by the St. Austell & Pentewan Railway on its eastern bank but now most traces of the railway have disappeared. *(The track was dismantled in 1918 and, along with the rolling stock, it was intended for use in France as part of the war effort. In actual fact, none of it left this country.)*

(Locomotive & General Railway Photographs)
National Railway Museum, York.
The West Hill, St. Austell terminus of the railway built by Sir Christopher Hawkins of Trewithen in 1829.

THE MILL - MOORLAND ROAD

The railway was laid on a raised track bed along Pentewan Road to Tregorrick, and part of the masonry walling can still be seen today, where it supports the footway beside the road. Bluebell Wood, mentioned earlier, lies behind the wall on the left of the picture. Moor Cottage stands behind the cottage reached by the cast-iron footbridge over the river.

The little railway, which ran from St. Austell to Pentewan, brought up coal, and staves for the coopers and carried china clay down to the port. Cement and corn were also handled at the port. The railway terminus at St. Austell was at the bottom of West Hill, where there was a weighbridge, two coal yards (Reeds and Truscotts), and clay stores or linhays. At first the engine hauled the trucks only as far as Tregorrick where there was a loop siding but no turntable, and from here the trucks were hauled to St. Austell by two horses and a driver - a Mr. Marks, who had no voice. He cracked his whip at me on a couple of occasions for riding on the buffers ! When the trucks were laden with clay, old Mac Grose used to stand on the front truck's buffers and apply the brakes when the trucks got to Tregorrick. They ran down to this point by gravity, and then the engine took over for the journey to Pentewan. I remember old Mac walking back to his home beside the track for his midday meal. There was a wooden rail bridge across the river into the mica-dry to enable the trucks to carry the dry clay out. As boys, the Tregorrick lads used to run out of school, along Moorland Road to the water wheel at the corn mill near the present health clinic, and then get on the buffers of the last truck to ride home. Old Mac never once stopped us ! Sometime later, the engine was permitted to pull the trucks all the way up to St. Austell. A boy was employed to wave a red flag when the engine crossed over the road at Tregorrick. The flag boys were Ben Solomon, Cecil Storey and Bob Huddy. Mr. Drew and his son were the engine drivers, Albert Storey was stoker and Vincent Powell was the track man. There were sidings into Gaved's yard, St. Austell, and at London Apprentice. I remember little about the Pentewan end of the railway, other than watching the sailing vessels being loaded and unloaded, the harbour gates being opened, and the ships being guided to the sea down the small channel which has now become silted up.

Courtesy of The Francis Frith Collection

Photographed just after the turn of the century, this postcard shows shipping in Pentewan Dock. On the left of the picture, railway wagons are standing on Iron Ore Quay, and on the right, clay is being tipped into a ship directly from a wagon rotated on a special device incorporated in the elevated trackway.

The "channel" between the dock basin and the sea which is now filled with sand almost to the level of the top of the quay. The construction of Pentewan Harbour was completed by Sir Christopher Hawkins in 1826. A commemorative "tablet", carved from Pentewan stone, just visible in the wall on the south-western side of the channel, depicts the coat-of-arms of the Hawkins family, and confirms the date.

(F. Moore's Railway Photographs) Ian Allan Group

"Canopus", 0-6-2ST, built by Manning Wardle in 1901, pictured on the elevated track at Pentewan. This engine was the third locomotive purchased for use on the St. Austell & Pentewan Railway. It replaced "Trewithen" in 1901, which had superseded the original locomotive "Pentewan" in 1886.

(F. Moore's Railway Photographs) Ian Allan Group

"Pioneer", 2-6-2ST, built by Yorkshire Engine Co., was purchased secondhand in 1912, probably as a standby to "Canopus", and is seen here at Pentewan coupled to the Hawkins family coach.

The principal landowners in the valley were Sawle (Penrice), Shilson (Trewhiddle), Tremayne (Heligan), Coode, Carlyon and, also, the Earl of Mount Edgcumbe. Those with residences in the area employed large numbers of staff, both indoor and outdoor, and also their own masons and carpenters. I particularly remember the staff at Trewhiddle House. When I was a boy, the staff there comprised cook, butler, footman, lady's-maid, kitchen maid, housemaids, chauffeur, five gardeners and one cowman, and sometimes extra casual workers were taken on for outside duties. These times are gone and are largely forgotten.

Heligan House was a convalescent home for wounded officers during the First World War.

Sir Charles Sawle's Penrice estate employed four gamekeepers and I remember there being two Pheasant Shoots a year there.

There was a cider press at Moor Cottage and another one at Treleaven's Farm at Nansladron and there were four slaughterhouses in the valley, namely, Jimmy Stephens' in Watering Lane, Fred Cole's at Tregorrick, Johnnie Hodge's at London Apprentice and Tucker's at Pentewan.

Johnnie Hodge and his daughter, Gladys, photographed c.1907 in the doorway of the Post Office at London Apprentice. The Post Office was situated opposite the pair of cottages on the northern side of the Chapel and it was demolished in the early 1980's to enable road widening to take place.

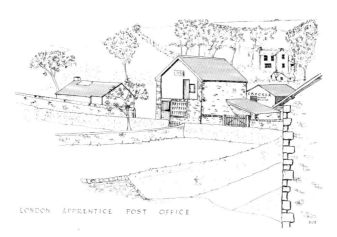

LONDON   APPRENTICE   POST   OFFICE

Moor Cottage, or White House, is owned by the Coode family. This family also owned other large properties in the town such as Trevarthian House and Pondhu House. I have been told that the Royal Cornwall Show was held at Moor Cottage in 1874. Two lodge cottages existed on the south side of the gateway to Moor Cottage.

At Menagwins was the old St. Austell Volunteer Rifle Brigade shooting range, with its butts in a field to the north of Molingey. The remains of the old ammunition house still stand on a bank between a stream and the former mill leat that supplied water to power the former mill at Molingey Farm, now converted to a dwelling.

In London Apprentice, there was at one time a mica works, where water was taken off the White River and allowed to settle in large tanks before the residue was dried in a large clay dry. When the mica works ceased, the site was used as a brickworks. *(This site is currently occupied by Mount Caravans.)*

There was a blacksmiths shop at London Apprentice, as I mentioned earlier, opposite the road turning to Polgooth, and there was another one near the narrow bridge over the White River at Pentewan.

In more recent times, there was a stream-tin works at Rosehill, London Apprentice, but this has now been returned to pastureland.

There were often serious floods in the Pentewan valley when the low-lying fields would be covered with water and mica which overflowed from the White River. Fortunately, since the river banks were straightened and the channel widened in the early 1960's flooding no longer occurs.

Many years ago, three men - a "captain" and two labourers, one of whom was my grandfather - were employed to maintain the banks of the White River and to keep its bed free from the build-up of sand from the china clay works. When the bed of the river became choked with sand, it was then the responsibility of the landowners adjacent to the river to have it cleared.

95

Harry Stark

The former mica works at London Apprentice were immediately north of Shepherdshill Bridge over the White River on the site of an earlier lime kiln.

Harry Stark

Another view of the mica works looking south-east from London Apprentice. The gamekeeper's cottage to the former Penrice Estate can be seen on the left, with Shepherdshill Wood in the background.

I can recall that it was impossible to walk along parts of some roads because of flood water, and it took quite a while for workmen with horses and carts to clear the roads after the flooding. I think the worst flooding was in 1903; the roads then were made up of stones laid down with a steam-roller and "bound" with earth. Consequently, they could not withstand the pressure of water and considerable damage was caused. In my young days, Mr. Blight was the road surveyor and he drove around with a pony and trap to do his work. There used to be piles of stones heaped up beside the roads. These stones were later broken up into smaller sizes by men who knelt all day cracking them with spalling hammers. The heaps were measured by the yard and placed into long, neat piles.

(Raphael Tuck & Sons)
Fine Art Developments Plc

A view down the Pentewan Valley towards Nansladron, showing a road-roller driver's wooden caravan, with its chimney smoking, and a pile of road chippings in a layby at Wood Orchard.

I remember the young men and women from Pentewan and Mevagissey riding their bicycles to St. Austell in all kinds of weather. In 1914, one could get a Raleigh bicycle for £7. I particularly remember Mr. Bob Evans who worked at St. Austell Brewery and who rode his bicycle from Pentewan every day to get to the brewery by 7.00 a.m. He was so punctual, one could set one's watch by him !

These notes are a nostalgic reminder of my younger days in and around St. Austell, where I have lived all my life, and I hope that the reader, too, may be pleasantly taken back to those "good old days".

THE "HORSES - DRINK" NEAR LONDON APPRENTICE

This simple facility enabled horses and cattle on the road to drink from a stream in an adjacent field. It exists exactly as it was built and has received minimal maintenance over the years, but the level of the road has been raised by approximately two feet.

"Good-Night!"

While strolling home one evening
Down the old Pentewan road,
I met a jolly Cornishman
Who whistled as he strode
With swinging gait, to pass me
In the deeply shadowed light;
And, as he passed, to wish me
A cordial "Good-night."

"Good-night!" said I, reflecting
As his footsteps died away -
Now what prompted him to say
"Good-night" to me so heartily,
As though he knew me well ?
Perhaps he did: on country roads
At night 'tis hard to tell.

But the world seemed all the brighter,
As I went upon my way,
For his cheery salutation
In the gloaming of the day.
'Tis a habit of the countryman
That rings supremely right,
This way he has of wishing
    All and sundry
    "Good-night!"

E.T. BOND

*(First Published in **Old Cornwall** - The Journal
of the Federation of Old Cornwall Societies,
Vol. V, No. 2, Summer 1952 .)*